Active Games for Children on the Autism Spectrum

Physical Literacy for Life

Erin Bennett, MAPA

Mary Dyck, PhD

HUMAN KINETICS

Library of Congress Cataloging-in-Publication Data

Names: Bennett, Erin, 1984- author. | Dyck, Mary, 1960- author.
Title: Active games for children on the autism spectrum : physical literacy
  for life / Erin Bennett, MAPA, Mary Dyck, PhD.
Description: Champaign, IL : Human Kinetics, [2024] | Includes
  bibliographical references.
Identifiers: LCCN 2022052119 (print) | LCCN 2022052120 (ebook) | ISBN
  9781718217171 (paperback) | ISBN 9781718217188 (epub) | ISBN
  9781718217195 (pdf)
Subjects: LCSH: Physical education for children with disabilities. |
  Physical education for children with mental disabilities. | Children
  with autism spectrum disorders--Education. | Movement education. |
  Autism spectrum disorders--Treatment. | Autistic children--Care.
Classification: LCC GV445 .B37 2024 (print) | LCC GV445 (ebook) | DDC
  371.9/04486--dc23/eng/20230109
LC record available at https://lccn.loc.gov/2022052119
LC ebook record available at https://lccn.loc.gov/2022052120

ISBN: 978-1-7182-1717-1 (print)

The web addresses cited in this text were current as of November 2022, unless otherwise noted.

Acquisitions Editor: Scott Wikgren; **Developmental Editor:** Jacqueline Eaton Blakley; **Managing Editor:** Anne E. Mrozek; **Copyeditor:** Chernow Editorial Services, Inc.; **Proofreader:** A.E. Williams; **Permissions Manager:** Laurel Mitchell; **Senior Graphic Designer:** Sean Roosevelt; **Cover Designer:** Keri Evans; **Cover Design Specialist:** Susan Rothermel Allen; **Senior Art Manager:** Kelly Hendren; **Illustrations (interior and cover):** Stephanie Webb-Addei; **Printer:** Color House Graphics, Inc.

Printed in the United States of America   10   9   8   7   6   5   4   3   2   1

The paper in this book is certified under a sustainable forestry program.

Human Kinetics
1607 N. Market Street
Champaign, IL 61820
USA

United States and International
Website: **US.HumanKinetics.com**
Email: info@hkusa.com
Phone: 1-800-747-4457

Canada
Website: **Canada.HumanKinetics.com**
Email: info@hkcanada.com

E8891

Contents

Teaching, assisting, and parenting children on the autism spectrum are rewarding and challenging tasks. Children on the spectrum are children first and foremost, with more similarities to nonautistic children than differences. Their bodies crave movement, their minds pursue interesting ideas, and they care deeply for those that support them.

Schools strive to be inclusive, but not all environments within schools are inclusive. Physical education and generalist teachers must manage their students' excitement while teaching physical literacy. Gymnasiums and other game-teaching spaces can create a challenging learning environment for children. The availability of educational assistants (EAs) may be limited. Many EAs, and teachers alike, feel underprepared to assist in the development of physical literacy for students on the autism spectrum. Physical education may give a child overwhelming anxiety. For this reason, some children are often left in a classroom or unused space, and physical education is replaced with another school subject.

Physical literacy is essential to a child's development of good health, a child's improvement in motor skills, and a child's growth in social skills. Therefore the purpose of this resource is to develop the courage, competence, and confidence required for helping children with autism develop physical literacy in ways that meet their unique needs. This book is principle based, with templates and lesson plans for ease of teaching. Teachers, EAs, parents, caregivers, and respite workers will benefit from the ideas presented and may seize the opportunity for providing hope and increased quality of life through physical literacy for children.

Chapter 1, Introduction, defines physical literacy. Autism spectrum disorder (ASD) is introduced, along with characteristics and considerations one encounters when teaching physical literacy. A reminder to use inclusive language provides a backdrop for this resource.

Chapter 2, Adapting Physical Activity, describes the rationale for and the how-to of adapting physical activity. Selecting the best environment is critical, whether the approach is to be one-on-one or full inclusion. The chapter provides an ADAPT decision flowchart to assist leaders in providing a framework for instruction, examples of adaptations and task progressions, and a chart for adapting with equipment.

Chapter 3, Planning, reminds readers that teaching requires planning for the unique needs of each child. This chapter includes helpful information on planning for communication and planning for the learning environment considering sensory needs, predictable routines, boundaries, and peer mentors. Strategies using consistent vocabulary, repetition, sequencing, prompting, and turn taking are explained. Motivation to participate in physical activity is sometimes of concern. This chapter presents strategies to increase motivation involving integrating interests, choices, goal setting, rewards, and reassuring control.

Chapter 4, Fundamental Movement Skills, encourages beginning in the early years to promote an understanding and enjoyment of physical activity. Chapter 4 supports the teaching of the fundamental movement skills that children need for a smooth transition to and in school and with physical activities in family and community settings. The fundamental movement skills begin with agility, balance, coordination, and speed (ABCs). Locomotor skills appropriate to this age include running, jumping, hopping, skipping, and galloping. A unique feature of this book is that it also defines the emerging skills of throwing, kicking, striking, catching, and trapping, as portrayed in stick figure images with instructional keys and feedback ideas for corrections. The text also describes a series of games that can be taught with one piece of equipment, with emphasis on the development of fundamental movement skills. The chapter concludes with a discussion of recess and playground activities.

Chapter 5, Physical Education and Community, continues the development of fundamental movement skills in school, family, and community-based programs. Many physical education lessons use sports and games to further develop physical literacy. Children apply fundamental movement skills and learn the basic strategies of games and sports. Children on the spectrum often avoid rather than engage in games and sports. The key to inclusion in physical education and games is a successful transition from one-on-one teaching to full class participation. The model Teaching Games for Understanding (TGfU) is presented to help children learn the principles of play. Teaching games according to common organization principles and tactics creates ease of understanding for students on the spectrum. The bulk of this chapter provides lesson plans and support for teaching the most common games and sports used in physical education today. There are also additional activities commonly used in community programs.

Chapter 6, Family and Friends, describes methods of teaching common physical activities enjoyed by family and friends. Step-by-step instructions are included to learn to bike ride, skateboard or scooter, swim, and ice skate.

Chapter 7, Fitness, provides instructional strategies and questions to ask at a community facility to reduce children's anxiety and encourage participation in fitness activities. Fitness training may be concurrent or in addition to school-based physical activity. Warm-ups, weight training, gaming, and outdoor equipment are discussed with the objective of enjoyment and a desire for lifelong physical activity.

Children on the spectrum are individuals first, who vary widely in skills, abilities, and the disposition toward physical literacy. Each individual is unique in the type of response that is required or helpful. Some children need a little more time to understand, a little more (and sometimes different) instruction, and a little more time to practice in order to develop movement skills and enjoy participation in games. The goal is for every child to be part of the physical education class, in the gym and on the field with their classmates.

This book is meant to be user friendly so teachers, EAs, and parents feel encouraged, confident, and competent in teaching children fundamental movement skills, game sense, and the enjoyment of being physically active for life. Have a plan to teach, take chances, keep thinking, be flexible, and be willing to try anything once.

Acknowledgments

Sometimes an idea comes to several people at the same time. The origin of this book is such a case. Several years ago, Sharryl Ochtabienski and John Byl began drafting a book on inclusive physical activity for children with autism. Simultaneously, the authors commenced writing a book on physical activity for children on the autism spectrum. In a chance correspondence, the ideas merged, and a decision to collaborate was made. We acknowledge the enthusiasm, effort, and contributions of Sharryl and John in the initial drafts. Sharryl contributed to the areas of characteristics of children, planning for instruction, and strategies for the early years in the current edition. John, as a veteran author, began as team leader and offered encouragement and insight. Dawn Campbell and Karen Steiner reviewed some of the original work and gave helpful advice for the fitness chapter. Thank you.

Thank you, Stephanie Webb-Addei, for your patience, creativity, and design skills in making the graphics.

Thank you to the Steadward Centre at the University of Alberta; without an introduction and experience in this world-class facility with its excellent staff, the area of adapted physical activity would never have become such an integral part of this journey.

Last, we acknowledge all children on the autism spectrum, their parents, and their caregivers, who allowed us the honor of working with them in physical activity. This also includes all of the schools, teachers, and educational assistants that welcomed us into their environment and gave us the opportunity to learn and develop these tools. Without this opportunity, the book would never have been written. You are the experts. We hope this book will give wings to your contributions so that all children may become physically literate for life.

Introduction

Meeting with a new group of students at a school is always an exciting experience for me as there are always nerves and anticipation for what will build and develop over the next school year. This group was full of characters, but one in particular stood out: Olivia, a sweet, timid girl on the autism spectrum. She, like me, seemed more interested in twirling in physical education class than playing a "sport." I have always tried to stay away from naming the sport we are doing and just call it a game because otherwise it puts a label on what we are to be doing with that certain piece of equipment (e.g., a soccer ball is only used for soccer, whereas a rubber ball can be thrown or kicked or struck or caught or carried or tagged in any number of games). Olivia participated well in all activities but was usually instructed hand over hand by her educational assistant. Throughout the year, she improved but still needed a lot of cueing. In the spring, her mother approached me about a summer activity for Olivia. She asked about a local soccer program and if I had any knowledge of it. With some information from the soccer program, I was able to figure out the basic skills that would be part of the program and what other activities were going to be done. Six weeks prior to the start of the soccer program I began introducing one soccer skill per session into the class. I used a regular ball and not a soccer ball, but we practiced kicking and stopping the ball, moving with the ball, shooting, passing with a partner, and passing the ball to a partner while moving. These activities didn't change my lesson plan or anything the rest of the class were doing, but they gave Olivia a chance to practice those skills before she attended the community program. It was great to see Olivia's skills progress and her overall confidence increase with just a few adaptations to the lesson plan.

Erin Bennett

Autism is complex, yet children on the spectrum have more similarities to nonautistic children than differences. Like all children, they enjoy movement, learning, and being supported by others.

Schools play an important role in the lives of all children. Physical education provides unique opportunities for student development; however, the environment may contribute to feelings of exclusion, frustration, and anxiety for teachers, educational assistants (EAs), and students. In many cases there are few EAs assigned to teachers, and sentiments of underpreparedness are common in teaching physical literacy and games for students on the autism spectrum. When children become overwhelmed in physical education, they often have physical education replaced with another school subject or are excluded from physical education with their peers.

The purpose of this resource is to develop courage, competence, and confidence in those living with, helping, and teaching children on the autism spectrum. Specifically, the ideas presented will benefit parents, teachers, EAs, caregivers, and respite workers. This resource is meant to give hope to educators and families and to increase quality of life by helping children become physically literate and enjoy games. A mantra for this resource is "more hopeful, less painful, less pointless."

This chapter first describes physical literacy and its relationship to physical education and games. Second, it presents a changing paradigm in autism spectrum disorder (ASD) from disability to difference. Third, autism is presented with the corresponding varying characteristics of children to consider when teaching physical literacy and games. Finally, positive word usage is presented to stop ableism.

Understanding Physical Literacy

Physical literacy is necessary for children to develop healthy bodies. Children who are physically literate demonstrate a variety of movements confidently and competently in a wide variety of physical activities (Haydn-Davies, 2005). Physical literacy is cyclic. When children are competent in their movements, they develop confidence in their movements and are more motivated to move. Figure 1.1 illustrates this cycle.

Physically literate individuals make healthy, active choices throughout their life span that are both beneficial to and respectful of their whole self, others, and their environment. Quality physical education programs provide the best opportunity to develop physical literacy in children and youth. After all, every child, regardless of age, gender, culture, socioeconomic status, or ability, goes to school. When children participate in

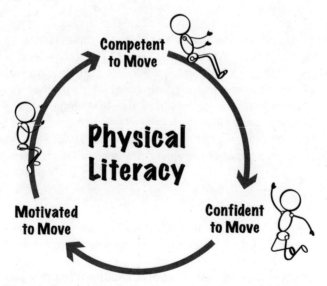

FIGURE 1.1   The cyclical relationship of competence, confidence, and motivation in physical literacy.

Adapted from "What is Physical Literacy," Physical Literacy, accessed December 1, 2022, www.physicalliteracy.ca/physical-literacy/.

quality physical education throughout their school years, they have the opportunity to experience a variety of activities in a progressive, sequential format that ensures maximum learning and enjoyment. Well-planned physical education programs complement sport-specific training and help to develop the skills and attitudes necessary for lifelong participation in games, sports, and physical activities.

Misunderstandings about autism continue to exclude children and youth from participating in physical literacy and activity programs (Cunningham, 2020). The lack of education and experience within the general population and the lack of training for leaders cause misconceptions regarding the ability of individuals and may result in lowered expectations for participation. Misconceptions may well result in individuals being excused or excluded from physical activity.

Differences may occur between children on the spectrum and nonautistic children, but those on the spectrum can achieve physical literacy similar to that of their peers (Johnson, 2004). Physical literacy and games benefit all children. Activity increases the ability to learn, improves cognitive performance, and promotes on-task classroom behavior (Trost, 2007).

Fundamental movement skills are the underlying abilities necessary to produce an action such as a jump or throw. Movement skills are fundamental to physical activity and sports. Children on the spectrum are capable of performing fundamental movement skills; however, many children have gross motor differences. A large majority of children on the spectrum do not display the appropriate motor skills of their age group (Hilton et al., 2012). Motion and movement are processed and perceived differently by the brain, leading to atypical gross motor patterns (Fletcher-Watson & Happe, 2019). One of the negative aspects of immature movement patterns and motor coordination differences is poor performance in physical activity settings. Children's participation in activities such as playing with their peers in parks, at school, in the streets, which supports the development of their communication and interaction skills, is also limited (Bhat et al., 2011).

In turn, children with motor differences run a much higher rate of bully victimization (Bejerot et al., 2011). A carefully and caringly constructed program of physical activity will help develop motor and social skills to increase inclusion in community life.

Other physical differences may include balance issues, hypotonia (muscle weakness), low manual dexterity, and overactivity. Many physical activities require the building blocks of balance, muscle strength, and manual dexterity. Differences with coordination, balance, and motor development may discourage children on the spectrum from even attempting to participate in physical activity. The most difficult movements require coordination of both sides of the body (such as galloping or skipping), require greater timing and coordination skills (for example, a layup in basketball), and where control of force or momentum is needed (bowling or batting are examples). All of these skills can be developed through involvement in physical activity and games with appropriate instruction, sequencing, and encouragement. Developing physical literacy will support inclusion in family, community, and school activities.

Community physical activities and recess times at school are vitally important to a child's overall health, development, and ability to learn. However, it is common for students on the spectrum to have lower levels of physical activity during unstructured recess times (Pan, 2008). Many things can be learned on the playground, such as how to get along, negotiate, make and follow each other's rules, talk to others, calm oneself, fall down and get back up again, and take turns. The opportunity to learn and practice self-regulation is another benefit of physical activity. With self-regulation comes more opportunity to be a part of family and community physical activities and games.

Families are the most influential agents in a child's development. Parents' beliefs, attitudes, and values regarding physical literacy and activity have a strong impact on which activities will be selected for the child (Lee, 2004). Children of parents who are physically active are more likely to be physically active. In preparation for school and beyond, families may need to provide additional activities to allow the child to make a smooth transition from home to school and community.

Therefore, physical literacy and games provide opportunities not only for health and development but also opportunities to improve areas of disadvantage unique to autism spectrum disorder. For children on the spectrum, physical literacy is especially important to improve their whole being—physical, cognitive, and social.

On the Autism Spectrum

Autism spectrum disorder (ASD) is a biologically based neurodevelopmental condition (Fletcher-Watson & Happe, 2019). Historically, ASD was classified as a severe developmental disability with challenges in social interaction, communication, imagination, sensory sensitivities, and restricted and repetitive behaviors (American Psychological Association, 2013). At present, there are no accurate prevalence measures (Fletcher-Watson & Happe, 2019). There are no reliable biological or behavioral markers to predict autism or determine cause (Muhle et al., 2018).

Today, autism is not characterized in terms of deficiencies or impairments but a pattern of differences, which present advantages and disadvantages in relation to nonautistic social norms and expectations. Differences can become disabling when they limit the person's activities, opportunities, and daily functions. Some experiences that typically accompany autism can be distressing and disabling, such as poor sleep, restricted diet, epilepsy, language delay, learning disability, and poor mental health (Fletcher-Watson & Happe, 2019).

Autism is a developmental difference that lasts throughout one's life. When viewed from the lens of neurodiversity, autism is conceptualized as a natural form of human variation, inseparable from an individual's identity and not in need of a cure or normalization (Kapp, 2020). Neurodiversity accounts for variability in brain structure and function. Cognitive processes account for the differences. The recent study of autism has been useful to understand the biological, cognitive, and behavioral levels (Fletcher-Watson & Happe, 2019).

On the biological level, autism emerges from differences in brain development due to a mix of common inherited genetic variations across many genes, each of small effect, and rare mutations of large impact. The integration of complex information from multiple sensory sources (visual, auditory, and tactile) is the task of the brain, and differences in brain development manifest as autism.

The cognitive (or psychological) level encompasses the processing of emotional information as well as the learning process and skills such as executive function, memory, and language. Levels of intellectual development vary greatly among children, and 50 percent of autistic children may have a learning disability (Fletcher-Watson & Kappe, 2019).

The emotional information process describes the everyday ability to recognize, represent, and interpret the emotional and mental states (such as beliefs and intentions) of others. Recognizing other states is different than thinking about why someone is displaying an emotional state. While there is some dissociation in autism, not knowing what others are thinking does not imply not caring. Attachment, empathy, and affection are not reduced in autism; therefore, this social difference involves feeling empathy versus expressing empathy. For example, a child on the spectrum may see their sibling get hurt and cry, but they may not rush over immediately to help because the situation may have become emotionally overwhelming. The child may leave the area or start exhibiting self-stimulating behaviors in order to calm down because they are upset that their sibling is upset. From the outside, it may appear that the child does not care or empathize with their sibling, but it may simply be how they express themselves or best cope.

On the behavioral level, autism consists of a constellation of traits that vary in presence, intensity, and function across individuals. A distinct feature of autism is an intolerance of uncertainty, sometimes referred to as "insistence on sameness" (IS) (Hundley et al., 2016, p. 349). *IS* refers to rituals, compulsions, excessive adherence to routine, and resistance to change in routines. Subsequently, the child may feel an overwhelming need for control. Without a sense of control, anxiety is amplified. A child can be physically aggressive or have outbursts when familiar environments or routines change.

Autism is therefore a way of being. It colors every experience, sensation, perception, thought, emotion, and encounter—every aspect of existence. It is not possible to separate the autism from the child—and if it were possible, the child would not be the same person.

Characteristics of Children and Considerations for Physical Literacy and Games

Children love to move. Developing physical literacy through physical education, community programs, and home activities provides many benefits. Considerations when planning and implementing games are communication, social interaction, specific interests, repetitive sensory motor behaviors, sensory sensitivity, emotional responses and self-regulation, and anxiety. Keep in mind that there is variance among autistic children.

Communication

Children on the spectrum may communicate differently than nonautistic children. Facial expressions, tone of voice, sarcasm, and jokes may not be understood because of a tendency to have a literal understanding of language. Children who are verbal may struggle putting sentences together. Echolalia is common, where the child repeats another person's words in an incorrect context (Lord et al., 2006). A flat, robot-like or high-pitched voice may be used, and the children may give unrelated answers to questions posed to them. Children on the spectrum may initiate or sustain a conversation and turn-taking within the conversation differently than the nonautistic child. The ability to communicate with others through verbal language, sign language, gestures, body language and facial expression, or assistive technology is necessary in almost any learning situation.

Social Interaction

Children on the spectrum may develop social relationships and enter social interactions differently than nonautistic children. Maintaining eye contact, interpreting and portraying facial and verbal expression, and responding with emotional reciprocity are part of the social differences. A difference in social skills does not mean that individuals do not desire social relationships.

Social rules and traditions may create disadvantages. Differences in social interaction often stem from an individual understanding and recognizing others' emotions differently than the nonautistic child. Children on the spectrum often struggle with interpreting the feelings, thoughts, and beliefs of others, and this can cause them to demonstrate different social behavior. Some behaviors may differ from social norms such that making friends is a difficult task. Actions of a person are governed by the information inferred from the other person's behavior and emotion, and application of those inferences within the social context is used to determine an appropriate reaction or behavior. The tendency of the individual to misinterpret the internal state or emotion of others or not to notice subtle signs can result in behaviors that are socially different than expected. Within the context of physical activity and games, differences may arise with how a child reacts to winning, losing, or criticism of performance. Physical activity can provide an opportunity for social interaction and social integration.

Specific Interests

Another difference of children on the spectrum is an intensity or focus on specific interests. This might include lining up objects and focusing on a part of an object, such as wheels (Johnson, 2004). Some children may focus their attention entirely on a theme (such as dinosaurs) and can relay an abundance of information about the theme. The development of these specific interests may be a result of autistic strengths of attention to detail, desire for order, and retention of information.

Repetitive Sensory Motor Behaviors

Often children on the spectrum will engage in repetitive sensory motor (RSM) behaviors (Gilchrist et al., 2018). RSM behaviors include the repetitive use of objects, complex motor mannerisms, and sensory-seeking behaviors. The children engage in behaviors in response to anxiety. These behaviors, commonly referred to as *self-stimulation* or *stimming*, are rhythmic and repetitive movements (such as hand flapping or rocking back and forth). Some may be self-injurious, such as head banging, hand biting, and excessive self-scratching or rubbing (Edelson, 1999). Stimming is often a request for reassurance, a response to changes in their routines, a reaction to highly stressful stimuli (too much noise), or a specific frustration. Stimming drowns out the anxiety and is often an outlet for negative energy. Stimming is a way of focusing on something the child enjoys while shutting out the overstimulation they experience in the real world. The child stimming may feel embarrassed. The other children may not understand what the child is doing or why they are engaging in different behavior. As children age, certain stims may go away or just change to something new. People deal with stress differently, and stimming is one way for children on the spectrum to deal with stress.

Sensory Sensitivity

Many children on the spectrum have different responses to sensory stimuli. Some children experience hypersensitivity (more than nonautistic children) to certain stimuli, whereas other children have hyposensitivity (less than nonautistic children) to specific stimuli. Different responses to touch, smell, sound, taste, sight, and feeling are typical sensitivities. Bright lights and buzzing from gymnasium lights can cause a child to become overstimulated and anxious, which is a disadvantage in a physical activity. The feeling of certain fabrics (like a shirt tag) against the skin may cause anxiety. Having a sensory sensitivity makes it more difficult for a child to be aware of their body in space, which makes it difficult to navigate space and obstructions in that space, stand at an appropriate distance from others, and even perform finite motions like tying shoelaces (Johnson, 2004).

Autistic children may experience hunger and pain differently (Fletcher-Watson & Happe, 2019). Some may have sensitivities to food and limit their diet to certain food only. A child on the spectrum may not show sensitivity to pain such as burns or bruises.

Physical activity and games are often performed in wide, open spaces, such as the gymnasium, a park, or a sports field. This environment may be disadvantageous for individuals on the spectrum. Many distractions and sensory stimuli are a part of almost any physical activity setting and are difficult to completely control. The field or gymnasium distractions include the amplification of sound, different activities occurring simultaneously, bright lights, and other visual stimuli. The activity itself may involve interpreting the movements and intentions of teammates or opponents, shouts or whistles, as well as multiple tactile stimuli. All these stimuli require simultaneous processing and comprehension, leading to overstimulation of a child or youth who may be hypersensitive to sensory stimuli. Due to the nature of physical activity, sensory overstimulation is a definite possibility; therefore, it is important to recognize that emotional reactions may occur and to prepare for them.

Emotional Responses and Self-Regulation

Children on the spectrum may respond to physical literacy and games in different ways. Some children will have outbursts as a result of their own frustration with themselves as they are unable to complete a motor task being taught or a reaction to complicated instructions. Behaviors such as bursts of temper, arguing, noisiness, or aggression may result from feelings of being overwhelmed. Physical activity provides individuals with many opportunities to develop self-regulation.

Anxiety

Another response to physical activity may be an apparent lack of attention or withdrawal. This reaction can also be a signal of anxiety or perceived overwhelming challenges the child is facing because of the activity (Adams et al., 2019). Receiving an overload of information, making mistakes as a new skill is learned, and long periods of listening to instructions can all be a part of a physical activity program and may lead to a child feeling overwhelmed, anxious, and uncomfortable. Some children are likely to react to challenges perceived as insurmountable with resignation (giving up) or avoidance. Physical activity could easily be perceived as frustrating; therefore, any physical activity should be presented in a manner geared toward success (no error teaching). There should be a focus on emotional security as a vital component when promoting any type of new (or old) physical activity or game.

Some of the core features of autism may act as cognitive barriers to physical activity, such as inattentiveness, narrow focus, and a tendency for adherence to routine. Feelings of frustration can quickly escalate if too much new information is provided or if there is a lack of structure. In reaction to frustration, participants are likely to disengage from the activity. Also, enhanced visuospatial skills of children on the spectrum may mean tiny changes in the environment cause anxiety (Fletcher-Watson & Happe, 2019).

Physical activity and games offer many social, emotional, and physical benefits to children on the spectrum. Although differences exist and needs must be met for children to participate in physical activity, there are methods that can be used to effectively reduce these disadvantages and provide the support needed for learning and enjoyment. The goal of physical literacy is for everyone to enjoy daily participation for life.

A Word About Language

Language is a powerful means for shaping how people view autism. Words may convey ableism. *Ableist language* refers to language, which assumes that people with disabilities or differences are inferior to nondisabled people. How people talk and write influences how people understand difference and disability.

Here are some suggestions to avoid ableist language (Bottema-Beutel et al., 2020, p. 3):

- Avoid the word *special*. Instead of *special interests*, use *focused interests*. Describe what the needs are rather than calling them *special*.
- Avoid using deficit language, such as *high functioning* or *low functioning*. Functioning varies across domains, time, and context and may depend on supports. Describe specific strengths and needs. Acknowledge the level of support required for specific areas and also note where minimal support is needed in other areas.
- Replace *treatment* with *support*, *services*, or *strategies*. Words such as *cure*, *recovery*, and *optimal outcomes* medicalize autism, and a better focus is on the quality of life that autistic people want for themselves.
- When referring to nonautistic people, avoid using *healthy*, *normal*, and *neurotypical*. *Neurotypical* assumes that nonautistic people are typical.
- *Challenging behavior* is value laden. Describe the behavior.

Awareness and usage of words can change the perception and acceptance of autism from a disability to a difference.

Conclusion

Human beings are made to move. Children require physical activity for healthy body development and require physical literacy to enjoy activity in school, in their communities, and with families. Tensions exist between the belief in finding a cure or need for rehabilitation versus improving the lives and community acceptance and support of those on the spectrum. For a child to learn and grow in school and community, there needs to be a middle ground. The voices of children on the spectrum must be heard while they learn fundamental movement skills, physical activities, and games. The goal is to assist in building the foundation for a long, healthy, active, happy life for all autistic children and their families.

In summary, children on the spectrum have a wide range of skills. For this reason, programs, instructions, and feedback need to be designed for the specific child or children with which you are involved. Be creative. Personalize the lessons, have courage to try, and have fun.

Working at a school for consecutive years allows me a greater chance to see how the students can develop and change over time. I met three boys on the spectrum who had good individual volleyball skills but lacked the ability to play as a group or in a team setting. Through the first year, we worked on basic skill development (practicing proper hand positions for basic contacts) and behavior in a physical education setting (not hanging off the net). The second year we worked on refining their skills by practicing aiming their shots and getting more height in their passes so the ball didn't hit the net. The third year we practiced small-group game passes in order to practice taking and waiting their turn with the ball. This was done by using lots of verbal cues and reinforcing good decision-making on the court. This example shows that developing the ability to play in a traditional game can take multiple sessions over multiple weeks or even years. It can take time, but the reward will pay off in the end!

Erin Bennett

CHAPTER 2

Adapting Physical Activity

Adapted physical activity is cross-disciplinary, practical, and theoretical knowledge focused on impairments, activity limitations, and participation restrictions in physical activity (*Definition*, n.d.). Adapted physical activity supports acceptance of individual differences, advocates access to activity for life and sport, and promotes innovative and collaborative service delivery, support, and empowerment.

The goal is to create an environment where a greater number of students will achieve success in the physical activity or education class. This doesn't mean that one teaches to the lowest skill level, but it means developing a lesson plan that allows for more skill levels to participate at the same time for a significant time of the class. Skills need to be developed within the class so that students progress in a way that keeps them motivated and engaged. In short, physical activities and games are adapted to allow participation, to allow inclusion alongside peers and within their families and community, to give hope to parents and caregivers, to reduce anxiety and increase enjoyment of activity, and to allow success in skill development. An individualized education plan (IEP) is an example of a plan that most schools would use in order to develop a teaching style and environment that would best suit the individual's needs and challenge them to develop and increase their skills in a variety of areas in education.

One of the ways to determine if adapting is necessary is to answer four questions when planning and leading the activity.

1. Is the learning environment safe?
2. Are the students engaged in the activity?
3. Do the students experience success in the activity?
4. Are the students developing skills?

(*NCCP Fundamental Movement Skills*, 2018 p. 53)

If "no" is an answer to any of the above questions, then there is a need to adapt for the activity. Four key principles will guide you in deciding how to adapt physical activities:

1. Identify the objectives for this unit or lesson. When a clear idea of the unit/lesson is known, one can begin to provide the adaptations that will meet objectives and develop physical literacy.
2. Maintain the integrity of the activity. This means that if the activity chosen is soccer, a ball-type object is kicked, and there is a goal area for scoring.
3. Challenge all participants regardless of skill level. Challenge is motivating and is the building block for improvement.

4.   Provide the best environment for learning. Several suggestions are provided in the remainder of this chapter.

Selecting the Best Environment for Developing Physical Literacy

When one is adapting physical activity, it is crucial to select the best environment for the child. The following sections describe environment options in order of most support to most inclusion in physical education or community programs. Keep in mind that there is much variation between students on the spectrum, and consequently, there are differences in support needs.

One-on-One Instruction

A one-on-one session is the most commonly used approach when teaching a child on the spectrum because they have been in similar situations from a young age due to speech, occupational, and physical therapy. One-on-one can be the easiest and most effective learning environment because it diminishes distractions and noise level. The leader can also control more of the environment and lesson. Skills can be worked on in a progression at the appropriate pace for each student. Remember that socialization is also an important skill to develop. This skill can be practiced in a physical activity setting by using a peer to practice skills that the student has been practicing with the leader. For example, overhand throwing with a partner or kicking a soccer ball back and forth is an effective and motivating method.

Small Group Instruction With All Adapted Activity

Using a small group can be beneficial because it incorporates a social aspect that is found in most physical education, physical activity group programs, and game settings. If the group can be made up of equally skilled students, it can be simpler to create a lesson plan because the students can then work together as a group to practice and increase their skill level while learning to play together. Because it is uncommon for all students to be of equal skill levels, one needs to lesson plan with a goal in mind and then plan two to three variations on how to achieve the same skill progressions for all those students. A template on adapting one common skill progression will be provided later in this chapter. An example of teaching in a small group with all adapted activity would be with Special Olympians. Participants in Special Olympics have developmental disabilities, and the organization's activities cater to that population in their teaching and lesson plan development.

Small Group Adapted Activity With Integration in Regular Physical Activity

This approach allows an individual or a group of students with differences to participate in a typical physical activity setting with necessary adaptations, such as equipment or support (whether it be a person such as an Educational Assistant [EA] or visual tools like a timer or visual schedule), to achieve success in the environment. Games and activities may be broken down, or students may be given extra practice time on a certain skill at the side of the playing area and then rejoin their classmates when appropriate.

Regular Physical Activity With Plans for Inclusion (no EA)

Depending on the level of support the student needs in a physical activity class, one can include a student within the regular class with small modifications. If the environment is set up to reduce distractions, the level of success is increased. If the student understands what is expected of them during the class, this can also add to the success of the class. One way to assist understanding is using visual schedules (for example, laying out the equipment needed for the class then putting away the equipment once that activity is done will allow the student to visually see how many more activities they need to complete in order to end the class). If the student has access to or is already using PECS (Picture Exchange Communication System) cards with the same equipment, the card can be taken off as completed. A timer can also be used in order to understand how much time is left.

ADAPT Decisions

Many teachers, assistants, and parents feel unsure when teaching physical literacy, fundamental movements, skills, or games. Many ask how one makes decisions and what influences the decisions. To assist in making decisions on how to adapt, a simplified flow chart for school, community, and family participation is explained (see figure 2.1).

The ADAPT decision-making flow chart begins with the leader (individual educational assistant, teacher, caregiver, or parent). First, the leader must consider the *internal and external personal factors* that will influence teaching decisions. Internal factors include one's own values and beliefs about inclusion; one's experiences with physical

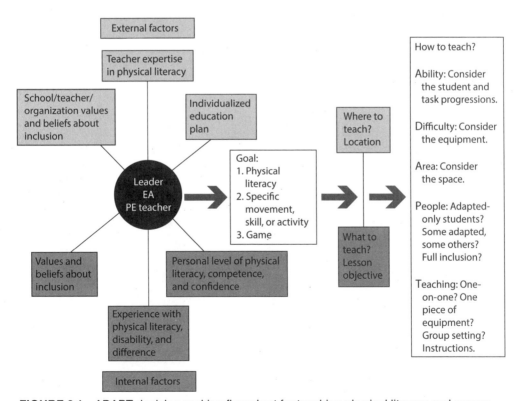

FIGURE 2.1   ADAPT decision-making flow chart for teaching physical literacy and games.

literacy, disability, and difference; and one's own personal level of physical literacy, competence, and confidence. External factors include the school, organization, and other teachers' values and beliefs about inclusion; teacher expertise in physical literacy; and the individualized education plan. Both internal and external factors form the context (positive or negative), which influences the leader's approach to the specific *goal* of the lesson. A typical goal of a lesson would be to develop physical literacy, to develop a specific movement or skill, or to learn to play a specific game.

Next is the question of where would be the best *location* to teach the goal. Realistically, there may be situations where not all children will be located together. While the goal is inclusion in at least part of the physical education lesson, another location may be chosen for the lesson. Be flexible and creative while still working toward the goal of inclusion.

After the goal and location have been chosen, the leader focuses on *what to teach*. What is the specific lesson objective, considering that a specific movement, skill, or game may be taught over multiple lessons? Some of the instructions and feedback from the next chapters will help the leader develop the actual activities for the lesson.

Lastly, the leader decides *how* to teach the specific lesson and how to ADAPT for the individual child or children in order for them to be successful, challenged, and included. The ADAPT model provides a framework for adapting physical activities and games. Using each letter of *ADAPT* as a reminder, one can quickly and creatively make adjustments to benefit the student, as shown in table 2.1.

The ADAPT model is applied to the following examples.

Individual Skill Example 1

Goal: kicking a ball

Ability: The skill of kicking a ball is an example of object propulsion. Break down the skill of kicking a ball by first introducing the skill of stepping in opposition. Place a sticker on the student's nondominant foot (ask which hand they eat with and then put it on the opposite foot). Place a polyspot or a line in front of the student and have the student step onto the spot or line repeatedly until the skill is mastered. Once a student can step in opposition, have them kick the ball with their dominant foot.

Difficulty: Begin with a larger, lighter ball and then increase difficulty with a smaller, denser ball or a ball used for a specific sport.

Area: Use a smaller space so that most of the time is not spent running and getting a ball. Increase the space size as the skill is mastered.

People: Begin with one-on-one instruction with either the student and an educational assistant, or you can pair the student with a peer but the idea of trapping the ball with their foot needs to be introduced if the peer and the student are to pass the ball back and forth.

Teaching: Try to encourage the slowing or stopping of the ball with feet only.

Individual Skill Example 2

Goal: skipping (five-year-old student)

Ability: A visual cue would be to put one sticker on each foot with opposite pictures (e.g., a dinosaur and a car). Then use the verbal cue of "dinosaur up" and "car up" in a sequence almost like marching.

Difficulty: Only stickers needed or if one has access to a trampoline this could add to the skill development.

Table 2.1   ADAPT Model

A	Ability	Adjust tasks and skills to match the students' abilities and interests. Determine the skills needed for the activity, such as locomotor or object propulsion or receiving skills. Break down the skills into their simplest components and develop task progressions.
D	Difficulty	Adapt the activity if it is too difficult or too easy. Often the equipment determines the level of difficulty. Equipment is the physical implement or protective clothing used in the game or activity. One of the easiest ways to allow full participation is using nontraditional equipment for the game. Adapt by changing the size, weight, shape, texture, color, or length or even the way the equipment is used during the activity.
A	Area	The physical space in which the activity is taking place either for the individual student or the whole group. Think shape and size. Increase or decrease the size of the playing field. Reduce the net or hoop or goal height. It can also include removing unnecessary equipment or noise from an area.
P	People	Determine if one-on-one, pairings, small group, or large group will lead to greater skill development and participation. Consider whether to match similar abilities together or have a good mix of abilities. Use more or fewer players on the court or field at a time. Break the group into smaller groups and have three games going on instead of one.
T	Teaching	Determine how to organize and instruct the individual, group, or class, including the rules for the activity. Use age and developmentally appropriate verbal and visual cues and language. Allow changes to the game rules of the activity or sport, such as more bounces, hits, or steps. Allow more time for the students to practice the skills.

Adapted from NCCP, "Fundamental Movement Skills," *Community Leader Workshop—Coach Workbook*, (Coaching Association of Canada, 2018), 53.

Area: Quiet space with an open space and limited distractions. Music may help but could be distracting for this skill.

People: One-on-one setting.

Teaching: Cue to move higher and higher to get one's knees up. Stand in front of student and then progress hand in hand beside the student moving around the area. Allow the student to take more steps in between the skips or allow for less air time in the skip.

Group Game Example 1

Goal: soccer (a group of grade 2 students with three students on the spectrum in an inclusive physical education class)

Ability: Play a game of soccer with the whole class and with all students on the field. Two students at a time serve as goalies, but switch out so everyone has a chance to be in goal.

Difficulty: Use a larger soccer ball, possibly an inflatable one, which provides a larger target for the students to kick and also allows more opportunities for each student to have a chance to kick the ball and be part of the game. Make the goal posts farther apart to allow for more opportunities to score. If needed, add another ball to increase the opportunity for participation.

Area: Use half of a gymnasium with a curtain dividing the gym. The other side also has a class taking place at the same time.

People: Since it is a physical education class, it may be impossible to split up the class into groups due to limited space. Split up the teams equally in terms of skill level.

Teaching: Allow for hands if needed to set up the ball by students on the spectrum. Add a rule that the ball must be touched by three different students before a shot can be made on the net if this allows more inclusion.

Group Game Example 2

Goal: basketball (grade 8 students in basketball at a recreation center with two students on the spectrum). This would be an introductory game for the whole group that could be used in the warm-up or could be transitioned later to a smaller group.

Ability: Slow the game down, and provide an understanding of purpose and flow of the game. Two teams are divided up equally, with each individual team member standing in their own Hula-Hoop moving up and down the court. All students stay in their hoop and move the ball up and down the court trying to aim at their respective basketball hoops. Running and moving around the court have been removed. Students need to pass effectively with their teammates since they cannot leave their hoops.

Difficulty: Equipment can remain the same as the game play is changed and slowed down, and given the age of the students, it is important to use a basketball and not another type of ball.

Area: A recreation center gymnasium, which could be loud or have higher sensory issues for the students; if the lights can be dimmed that would be ideal. If the basketball group is the only user group in the gym, it also reduces noise and distractions. If it is possible, have a quiet space outside the room, which can also help with any sensory issues if the student needs a break.

People: Two equal-ability teams. Group instructional setting with one assistant for both of the students on the spectrum.

Teaching: One team has the visual cue of pinnies.

These examples show how the ADAPT model works to tailor the activity for maximum inclusion and participation in physical activities and games. Another helpful teaching technique is task progressions.

Task Progressions

Task progressions involve breaking movements, skills, and games into the smallest possible ideas and building success from those ideas. As success is achieved, more pieces of the task are added until the student can achieve the objective and goal. Task progressions can be done through individual or group instruction. Examples of individual instruction and group instruction task progressions are provided next.

Individual Instruction

Table 2.2 is a template of a breakdown of teaching a single skill for an individual in a physical education game setting.

Table 2.2   Task Progression Example for Individual Instruction

Identify skill needing more practice	A child likes playing baseball with the class but isn't able to throw the ball with the force needed to get it to the infield.
Identify skill needed	Overhand throwing
	Practice stepping in opposition with nondominant leg. Exercise: Do this by having student step in front with nondominant leg onto a line or polyspot. Back foot remains on other line. Needs to become natural. Can use a sticker on shoe to give a visual reminder.
	Practice giving high fives with dominant hand. Exercise: Start doing high fives with dominant hand in close proximity, and then get farther and farther away (approximately after 5 repetitions) until the student is reaching for the instructor's hand.
	Practice stepping in opposition and giving high fives. Needs to become natural and move in one full movement with a smooth transition from the beginning position.
	Place a beanbag for an easier approach or a ball for a more advanced approach in the dominant hand of the student. Practice the whole sequence together with the implement in hand. Do not worry about accuracy or the distance the implement is thrown at this point. It is the fluidity of the sequence that is important.
	Continue to practice the sequence with a ball in order to improve distance and accuracy.
Fine tuning the skill for accuracy, consistency, timing	Set up Hula-Hoops to represent bases. Choose a distance target (far wall in the gym or tree outside). Add a batter to practice pitching, or place a student at second base to practice throwing to first and third base.

Task Group Instruction

Table 2.3 is a template of a breakdown of teaching a single skill to a group in a physical activity setting. When considering the skill or game objective, take the time to break the objective down into tasks from simplest through to complex or game speed.

Table 2.3 Task Progression Example for Group Instruction

Identify skill needing more practice by the group	Changing directions quickly in a group game
Identify skill	Pivoting off one foot then transitioning back into movement
Individual work	Place a polyspot or use a line on the floor in front of each student.
	Place a sticker on the student's dominant foot (a dinosaur works well).
	Cue the student to stomp on the spot or line. Use the verbal cue of "roar" every time they step on the spot.
	Then cue "go" and have the student point to the opposite direction and move in that direction. Students may cross their feet as they turn the wrong way, so emphasize that they turn the easy way and not the "hard" way.
Partner work (EA)	May need to instruct hand over hand if needed
Small group work	Play a game of ship to shore, with the polyspots or line as the ships and the shore. Have the students run back and forth between the two, and reinforce the pivot turn at the end (Ultimate Camp Resource, n.d.)
Fine-tuning the skill for accuracy, consistency, timing	Remove the spot or line as a visual cue.
	Increase the pace of the pivot in order for a quicker change of direction. Speed up the cue for the pivot, or do multiple pivots in a short time.

Adapting With Equipment

When adapting an activity for a child, consider how to make the skill easier or harder based on equipment characteristics. Object manipulation skills (sending and receiving) involve equipment. Table 2.4 shows the variability of equipment (Kasser & Lytle, 2013).

Table 2.4   Equipment Variability

Category	Increase Difficulty	Make Easier
Weight	Heavier	Lighter
Size	Larger	Smaller
Shape	Irregular	Regular
Height	Higher	Lower
Speed	Faster	Slower
Distance	Farther	Closer
Sound	Noisy	Soft
Color	Bright	Pale
Trajectory	High or low level	Medium level
Direction	Backward, sideways, left, right	Forward
Surface contact	Decrease	Increase
Surface or texture	Rough or uneven	Level or smooth
Length	Longer	Shorter
Resiliency	More	Less

Adapted from S.L. Kasser and R. Lytel, *Inclusive Physical Activity: Promoting Health for a Lifetime,* 2nd ed. (Champaign, IL: Human Kinetics, 2013).

Conclusion

All children want to enjoy physical activity and be competent and confident in their abilities. Leaders must select the most appropriate environment for learning. Motor proficiency takes time and practice. For children on the spectrum, aspects of teaching physical literacy and games may need adaptation. The decision chart, ADAPT method, and examples are presented in this chapter to help leaders adapt physical activity for success and enjoyment by children.

CHAPTER 3

Planning

Effective teaching begins with planning. Teachers and leaders not only plan the content of physical literacy and games but also must consider the learning environment. Physical literacy and activity programs need to provide a strength-based environment of difference and deliver the content where a culture of diversity is the norm (Humphrey & Lewis, 2008). Each child on the spectrum is a different child, though there are similar strengths and disadvantages. One must see teaching through a different lens. The activities and structure must help students positively embrace their ability and help them to reduce negative feelings of low self-esteem and self-doubt that feeling different can bring (Cunningham, 2020).

This chapter provides ideas for planning of physical literacy and games. First, all teaching and learning environments rely on communication. Children communicate in different ways. Second, several important areas are presented to facilitate planning the environment where learning has an optimal opportunity for development. The third section gives helpful directions for giving instructions, consistent vocabulary, repetition, sequencing, and prompting. Turn taking requires careful planning to reduce anxiety. Motivation is the fourth area to be covered, with many suggestions to encourage and sustain effort. The next section provides behavior management examples and solutions. Understanding the root cause of behaviors allows leaders to calm anxious children and provide strategies for reducing recurrence. The chapter concludes with a discussion on reducing anxiety by giving the child a sense of control.

Communication

Physical activity often requires interactive communication. Various methods can be used to address the communication needs in a physical activity setting. Some children may use their voice, whereas others will communicate through pictures, sign language, or technology tools. All children use body language to communicate. Keep in mind that a nonverbal child may very well understand all that is being said.

Individual Communication and Body Language

Each person has developed their own way of expressing themselves. Some children are unable to communicate effectively with verbal language. Careful observation will allow one to understand the body language and other signals that individuals use to communicate their emotions, thoughts, and needs. Families and friends of the child will have an advantage over others in understanding the individual and can be a great source of assistance for the leader.

Picture Exchange Communication System

A child's communication needs may be met by using a Picture Exchange Communication System (PECS) or a similar communication device or application. The PECS is a communication tool that encourages the development of spontaneous expression and conversation skills. It allows the individual to make a request or initiate a conversation rather than only answering questions. In PECS, the child identifies a desired object or activity in a picture and gives the leader the picture in exchange for the item or activity (Allen et al., 2011). PECS can be individualized so that each person has their own collection of picture words or sentences that they can use to communicate and express their needs. There are also many applications for a tablet that are based on PECS.

Sign Language

Some children communicate through sign language. Teach basic sign language that is used in physical activity settings (sit, stand, go, stop, run, more, finished, yes, and no) (Rouse, 2009). Peers can use these basic signs as well. Teaching sign language does not discourage children from finding their verbal voice. It is helpful to say the words with signing, such as showing the sign and saying "play." Doing both enhances learning and understanding the meaning of the sign. Teaching simple but powerful words makes a huge difference in the child's ability to communicate, and it reduces frustration.

Assistive Technology

Communication tools assist children to achieve education, learning, and life-skill goals. Touch screens, tablets, and handheld computers are appealing to children due to their multisensory nature with images, sound, and vibration. Some of the benefits of using assistive technology for communication and other needs include the following:

1. Children have the same tools and technology as other children. Children, instead of appearing different than their peers, can now be more similar and accepted.
2. Children have increased motivation to understand, stick with, and complete tasks using technology tools.
3. Children have shown a desire to initiate activities with other children using touch-based tools.
4. Educational and fun games can also be downloaded onto the same device to be used as positive reinforcement for effort or completed tasks, behavior management, and rest periods. Children can also shut out noise or listen to music without disturbing others.

Communication is a foundation of the learning environment. Find the preferred method for the child and start there. Use friends and families as allies to help you best understand and communicate with the child.

Planning for the Learning Environment

The environment sets the stage for learning to take place. The primary goal is to understand and provide opportunity for the development of physical literacy and games. A secondary goal is to create an optimal environment for children on the spectrum that leads to greater autonomy and self-determination (Green et al., 2017). This section provides ideas related to the environment, such as addressing sensory sensitivities, developing predictable schedules, setting boundaries, and using peer mentors.

Sometimes, factors relating to the child outside school may affect learning for a particular time and day. The following are some questions to consider about the student before heading into a physical activity setting:

- Has the child not slept the night before or been up since very early this morning?
- Does the child have any bowel issues (e.g., not having a bowel movement in a number of days) or any other gastrointestinal issues?
- Has the child started a new medication or new diet?
- Has there been a new educational assistant or teacher in the child's life?
- Has there been a change in the child's home life? After school care?
- Has the child started a new therapy? Changed therapists? (Speech/PT)?
- Is the child wearing new shoes or a new clothing item?
- Has the child eaten today?
- Does the child have a comfort item (toy, object, fidget toy, picture of favorite character, chewable item) with or near them?
- Did the child arrive to school on time? Was their transportation any different today?
- How was the morning transition or school transition disrupted today?

Any changes or struggles in the life of the child on a given day may affect how the child responds in a physical activity session. Be aware and have a backup plan for common challenges.

Sensory Sensitivities

Some children on the spectrum will be hyperstimulated by their senses (noise, touch, temperature, lighting). Here are some suggestions to reduce the overstimulation triggered by environmental factors of physical activity. First, organize the space to reduce the feelings of exposure that may result from large, open spaces. Pylons, curtains, or barriers all are effective tools. Reducing stimuli, such as dimming the lights, turning off music, providing earplugs, and removing distractions from the perimeter of the activity area can also effectively reduce overstimulation. Offering the individual a safe place that they can escape to and reorient themselves can be a successful way to overcome the barrier of environmental overstimulation. An activity such as a stationary bike that is safe and appealing to the individual or just a small area that promotes relaxation are examples of safe zones that can be created.

Sensory sensitivities may cause high levels of anxiety. When anxious or overwhelmed, a child may display self-stimulating behaviors (stimming). This repetitive behavior is hard for the individual on the autism spectrum to control, and although some behavior may be calming to the person, it does interfere with learning and making friends. Touch is another sensory stimulus that some participants may not tolerate.

Other participants will have hypoactive senses (underresponsive) and can become self-injurious when frustrated or anxious (e.g., engage in head banging, biting, or scratching). It should be noted that the responses to over- or understimulation are from the same cause, but they have a different manifestation.

Sensory difficulties may present a disadvantage for a new participant in an activity program. Participation can begin in steps, for example, come to the area, sit on the perimeter of the activity, participate in the first activity or warm-up, and eventually participate in all activities. Each participant may be different in how long they spend at each step. The leader must allow time and modifications for success at each step (Rouse, 2009).

Table 3.1 provides ideas for addressing behaviors that may occur in a physical activity or game session.

Table 3.1 Approaches to Address Behaviors in a Game or Activity

What behavior?	What to do?
Stimming from over-stimulation	• Slow down the activity. • Take the person aside. • Use a timer. • Walk the perimeter of the activity area. • Let the student go to a safe area in the activity venue.
Self-injurious stimming	• Intervene and stop the activity. • Add an alternative activity. • Let the student go to a safe area in the activity venue. • Leave the area.
Touch sensitivity	• Replace holding hands or tagging with a ring, rope, pool noodle, or an item of their choice. • The child can give a verbal or hand signal when not available to be touched or tagged.
Anxiety from new activity in the venue	• Begin in steps. Different children will require different lengths of time in each step. • Come to the area. • Sit on the perimeter. • Participate in the warm-up or first activity. • Gradually add participation length and engagement.
Anxiety from too much in the activity	• Instruct the child to focus on only one sensory stimulus at a time (e.g., the ball in a soccer activity).

Predictable Routines

Predictability and routine help to alleviate feelings of anxiety. Daily and weekly timetables and activities are written and clear with concise instructions. Careful planning transitions between stations is also needed (O'Connor et al., 2000). Establish and maintain a predictable environment; the leader's language and behaviors, session schedule, location, furnishing, and equipment contribute to an optimal learning environment (Allen et al., 2011).

There are several ways to establish predictable routines within sessions, including visual schedules, timers, countdowns, and social stories.

Visual Schedules

A visual schedule is a primary component of a structured learning environment when working with children. It can help with increasing "sequential memory" and having a better understanding of time organization, language comprehension, and leader expectations. It can also be helpful in transitioning a child from one location to another. Visual schedules are useful tools that allow a child to better comprehend their day, the tasks ahead, and what is being asked of or expected from them. They can also lessen the anxiety that the child may experience and thus decrease uncontrollable behaviors.

Typically, a visual schedule is a list of activities (pictures or words) that the child carries or the leader displays for the child. It allows the child to identify tasks, and as tasks are completed they can be removed from the schedule. The activities may be written in erasable markers or be attached by Velcro, thus allowing the child to easily erase the activity once completed. Visual schedules can also be on a tablet or phone, which allows a sense of regularity for the participant because it is commonplace to carry a cell phone or tablet around in day-to-day activities. A visual schedule can be made up with the equipment that will be used in a particular session. The child can know what is first, second, and so on. Each time equipment is used, it can be put away, and the child knows what is next and also when the lesson will be done.

A visual schedule can be used for outlining a single task (e.g., kicking a ball) or something more complex, such as aiding in participation in a physical education class. This can allow for participation more easily as the leader or educational assistant can program a schedule that allows for maximum participation in the class or activity while allowing for scheduled breaks in order to decrease anxiety. When the child has the skill or game broken down into individual tasks it becomes less overwhelming, allowing for greater success in a physical activity setting.

A preferred activity or reward tends to be given (depending on the motivation of the participant) at the completion of the tasks on the visual schedule in order to reinforce compliance, positive behaviors, or participation in activities completed. Physical education, fitness, or games may not be of interest to the participant, but a reward at the end of the schedule may increase the completion of the tasks more quickly. For example, a young student who does not enjoy playing games can be rewarded for participating with their peers in group games with three minutes of playing time (interactive games or music) on a handheld device or tablet.

Visual schedules are a critical component of teaching children and youth in a physical activity setting. With new programs and multiple applications available for little to no cost, the leader may communicate more effectively, which will then allow for children's greater understanding, reduced anxiety, and enjoyment in their lesson.

Timers and Countdowns

Timers and countdowns allow for a visual cue that indicates the remaining time for an individual to complete an activity, exercise, or game. Timers generally count up, and countdowns will count down to the completed time. Leaders can verbally and visually count down or up to prepare individuals—for example, "In 10, Sam will kick the ball: 10 9 8 . . ." (using fingers to indicate this as well).

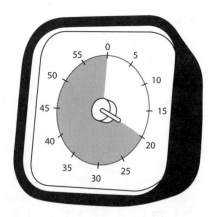

Since individuals thrive on routines and structure, having a timer available in the session allows the individual to feel in control of the situation and reduces stress. Some individuals may feel stress when they do not have a set schedule, and by giving each activity a time limit, stress is reduced. Another benefit to a timer is that it can also function as a turn taker. Taking turns allows individuals a chance to work on a needed social skill. Timers that are developed with taking turns in mind can help show the individual how much time they have left in a turn or how long until it is their turn again. More information on turn taking is in the section on Planning for Teaching Physical Literacy and Games.

Social Stories

The goal of social stories is to share accurate social information in a calm and reassuring manner that can be easily understood so that the individual has an improved understanding of events and social expectations (*What Is a Social Story?* 2022). Social stories are effective in preparing the participant for physical education class or community recreation programs because these are environments that tend to be noisier and less structured due to other participants in the class and the nature of the instruction of the program. A social story can help the participant understand and be prepared for what can happen in these environments, which can lead to inclusion in physical activity. Social stories can describe a situation, skill, or concept in terms of relevant social cues, perspectives, and common responses in a formal, specific, defined style (*What Is a Social Story?* 2022).

The following three steps describe how to make a social story:

1. Plan the social story.

    First, determine if a social story would be appropriate for a particular participant. The purpose is to promote an appropriate behavioral response rather than having to tell the participant what not to do. The story must be concise and interesting.

2. Develop the social story.

    Gray (2004) recommends that the beginning of the story must identify the topic, the body provides additional information about the social situation, and the conclusion restates the topic. Include all the who, what, when, where, why, and how. Provide socially relevant cues to help improve the participant's understanding of the social situation and increase the likelihood of a desired response.

Pictures should support the text in a meaningful way. Video can be used in a digital social story. Write the story in the first person. Avoid the word *not*. Be consistent with the story. Include only enough information to increase understanding and comfort, not everything that might occur in the session (Rouse, 2009). Write stories about skill development and participation first and then behavior modification if needed, because this sets a more positive tone.

3.   Implement the social story (Sandt, 2008).

Read the story before the participant is in the social context. The story can be read frequently for maintenance of behavior. The story should be read when the participant can engage. It should not be read when the participant is upset or as a result of uncontrollable behavior.

4.   Here is an example of a social story.

My name is Sam.

Today in PE I will play basketball with a big ball.

Sometimes I will hold the basketball in my hands.

Sometimes I will dribble the ball.

Dribbling means to bounce the basketball on the ground with my palms.

When it is my turn I can dribble the ball.

I will try to wait my turn in line.

Sometimes I will pass the basketball.

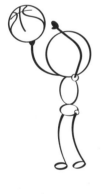

Passing means to bounce or throw the ball to another person.

I will try to pass the ball to other people.

I will also try to catch the ball when other people pass it to me.

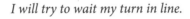

When I am close to the basket, I will try to shoot.

When it is my turn I will try to do what the other kids are doing.

When the leader is talking, I will listen.

I will have fun when playing basketball.

Adapted from P. Rouse, *Inclusion in Physical Education*, (Champaign, IL: Human Kinetics: 2009).

Setting Boundaries

Polyspots are helpful to set boundaries in group activities and encourage staying on task. By having a consistent polyspot for the beginning and during each activity, the child knows where to be. Each child can have a different-colored spot, and this allows easy communication and direction. Peer mentors can redirect a child back to their spot if needed. Having a spot reduces running aimlessly around the activity area and helps the child to focus. Along the same idea, providing an area that is a safety base in games creates a secure boundary where other participants are restricted from entering and can increase participation and enjoyment and reduce anxiety.

Peer Mentors

Other people's reaction to the social and communication differences that children and youth on the autism spectrum display can often lead to isolation or rejection. One way of overcoming segregation and misunderstanding is to incorporate peer mentors. A peer mentor can act as an example to others by showing them how to develop a relationship with someone on the spectrum.

Many of the program ideas in this book include the important use of peer mentors. Peer mentors are able to help others, be active, get healthy, have fun, and be an important peer model to others (Ochtabienski, 2012). The ultimate goal is to bring everyone together and enjoy physical activity. Peer mentors are taught techniques and patience to help their peers in need of some extra attention. Children learn leadership skills, empathy, and the willingness to understand and accept children that may be different from themselves. This program is beneficial to both nonautistic children and those on the spectrum.

Peer mentors can play an incredibly positive role in each other's lives in ways that parents, leaders, and therapists cannot. Children are accepted and learn in integrated settings from others their age (Ochtabienski, 2012)

In summary, planning for the learning environment is the first step in addressing the needs of children on the spectrum. When the environmental disadvantages are reduced, so will the anxiety be reduced for the children. The leader can now focus on planning how to teach physical literacy and games.

Planning for Teaching Physical Literacy and Games

Planning bridges the idea of a lesson to the necessary considerations for teaching the lesson. Once the learning environment is optimal, the leader must plan how to teach. This section provides suggestions for giving instructions, using consistent vocabulary, benefiting from repetition, sequencing, and prompting.

Giving Instructions

Instructions should be clear and concise, using one or two simple instructions. Abstract thinking is sometimes a difference between nonautistic and autistic children. Care should also be taken to avoid metaphors and nonliteral expressions. Speaking in the third person can be helpful for a child who reverses pronouns.

When instructing, give verbal or visual directions or both, but not at the same time, and allow extra time for the student to respond. A simple strategy for prompting and remembering the delayed response time is "tell, show, do." Tell the child what you want him or her to do, wait five seconds, then show the child what to do, wait five seconds, and do or physically assist the child in performing the task (Rouse, 2009). More on prompting appears later in this section.

Using consistent language is very important. Use one word for *stop* or *freeze* but not both. Encourage communication with words, and include hand signals to give a means for answering (e.g., the participant can touch your right hand for "yes" and your left hand for "no" or use the appropriate sign language).

Consistent Vocabulary

A consistent vocabulary and key phrases help to organize social interactions. Most social situations have a structure to them. There is a beginning, a middle, and an end. This structure allows those interacting with one another to understand where they fit into the interaction and where the interactions are moving (Ochtabienski, 2012).

When developing activities for children it is important to establish structure and give them an understanding of what to expect and when to take their turn. By using a consistent vocabulary and key phrases to begin the game, keep the game going, and put an end to the game, the leader can help the child remain on task. Key phrases need to be kept simple, clear, and consistent. Once the child has learned these verbal prompts and is successful with turn taking, one can begin to use the same vocabulary to structure new games and activities. By using the same words and applying them to a variety of games, the stress put on a child is lessened, even when they are learning something new. Another bonus is that this technique gives them more confidence to become involved in something different. Trying anything new can be a great source of stress to children. Keep the game the same as much as possible, and gradually introduce minimal changes. Too much change all at once will often result in immediate rejection of the activity and escape behavior.

Table 3.2 shows some examples of how to set up a consistent vocabulary when planning activities.

Table 3.2   Using Consistent Activity Vocabulary and Phrasing

Beginning	Hello class.	Let's warm up.	
	Hello class.	Let's _____.	Jump, run, hop, skip.
	Hello class.	Let's play ____.	Tag, catch.
	Hello class.	Let's play with____.	Noodles, balls.
Middle	Nick's turn first.	Susy's turn next.	
	Whose turn is it?	Nick's turn.	Good job, Nick.
	Whose turn is it?	Susy's turn.	Good, job, Susy.
Ending	Give time warning.		
	All done.	Finished.	
	Clean up.		

From S. Ochtabienski, *A+ Activity,* (Unpublished manuscript, 2012).

Repetition

Learning requires repetition. Tasks should be broken down to their simplest form and practiced until mastered. Students should be successful at 70 to 80 percent of the attempts. Five repetitions allow for easy calculation of 80 percent of mastering the skill. A student should perform the task correctly four out of five times with no prompting at least three times before moving to a new task (Ochtabienski, 2012). The student can then move on to the next skill or step, which is linked to the first step. Steps are linked as they are mastered until the full task is complete. Therefore, the process of learning a new task can be short or very lengthy depending on the difficulty of skills and number of steps required. Repetition sets the base for sequencing and acquiring the whole task.

Sequencing

Sequencing is required for all tasks and increases the ability to complete more advanced or complicated tasks. Sequencing is a required skill for executive function and cognitive learning. Early examples are learning the alphabet and counting. Sequencing is also required to learn motor skills and to advance to more mature movements. Sequencing teaches children how to follow directions, starting at a one-step task. The child then advances to two-step directions, and then three steps, and so on.

Prompting

Table 3.3 shows prompting techniques used to help children with language development, performing tasks, and communicating with others. The types have been placed in order from those children requiring full prompting to fading out the prompting; from more intrusive to less intrusive.

Turn Taking

All children have a hard time taking turns. Young children are developmentally self-centered. As children get older they are taught social rules on how to share, wait, and take turns playing with their peers. Some children on the spectrum may not understand the social rules. The children may also lack the motivation of wanting to play with others (Ochtabienski, 2012). They do not see the nonverbal communication that another child is trying to make. Their opportunities to develop social interaction skills are hindered because they reject other children's attempts to interact, and they disrupt planned activities. Children on the spectrum must be exposed to situations where they have to interact with others to function in natural social settings. Turn taking requires the child to stop what they are doing to allow the other person to have their turn. The child also needs to be able to accept the result of their turn, which they may not always view as positive. Another common characteristic of those on the autism spectrum is that they must do the task correctly. If their turn did not go well, or so they think, they need to do it again and again until they get it right. In most cases, failure to have more turns may lead to frustration and uncontrollable behavior.

Practice taking turns when playing simple games or doing simple tasks. Choose a piece of equipment that the child enjoys. Take turns doing a simple activity like squeezing a

Table 3.3 Prompting Techniques

Type	What is it?	When to use?	Example:
Full physical prompt	Leaders use their hands to move the child's body through the range of motion or skill.	Child is developing motor skills. Allows a feeling of performing the task.	Use hand over hand to catch.
Partial physical prompt	Leaders use their hands to initiate an action or remind the child how to make the motion or skill.	Child is comfortable with the complete motion, less fearful of the sensations, and muscles are starting remember the motion.	Tap knee to initiate bending to jump.
Model prompt	A leader or other participant provides an accurate demonstration of a complete or partial movement or skill.	Child can see a model and process the image and movement with a similar attempt.	Leader demonstrates kicking a ball in regular and slow motion.
Picture prompt	Leader provides an accurate picture of complete or partial movement or skill.	Child can connect the picture(s) to performing the movement or skill.	Show picture of the phases of striking a tennis ball with racquet.
Full verbal prompt	Leader gives verbal commands or cueing to develop or improve performance. Includes: skill cues, action commands, and action cues.	Child needs to learn the language linkages between the words and the movement or skill.	Skill cue: Swing your arms. Action command: Jump down. Action cue: 1, 2, 3, go.
Partial verbal prompt	Leader provides incomplete verbal commands or cueing to continue the development of movement or skills.	Child has some verbal skills and needs to further build the linkages.	_____, set, go.

Adapted from L.E. McClannahan and P. Krantz, *Activity Schedules for Children with Autism: Teaching Independent Behavior,* 2nd ed. (Bethseda, MD: Woodbine House, 2010).

rubber animal or bouncing a ball. Set a timer or set a number of repetitions that each person can do with the favorite piece of equipment.

Motivation

A concern of individuals and the parents of children on the autism spectrum is a lack of motivation to be physically active. Challenge increases motivation, and vigorous activity keeps children on task. To increase the appeal of physical activity, some ideas include integrating the interests of the child to make it meaningful, giving choices, using "first this, then that" strategy, utilizing the child's preferred movements, setting goals, using token boards, and giving meaningful rewards (including rewards that exist outside the actual physical education class). Time on tablets or any stimming products can be rewarding and motivating to the student.

Integrating Strengths or Interests

Some children are attached to particular types of objects that serve no apparent function but intrinsically provide enjoyment for them. These objects may be used to motivate the child to perform a skill, either by rewarding the child with time to play with the objects after compliance or by incorporating the object into the activity. For example, adding memory or math skill components or favorite animals to a physical activity may increase success and result in increased motivation.

Choices

A choice can be provided, whether in choosing equipment or the activity, so that the child has a sense of control. For example, "Sam, which ball would you like to throw to your friend? The red ball or the blue ball in your hand?" (Yanardag et al., 2010). Another method for improving adherence to an activity is to use the phrase, "MY Choice, YOUR choice." The leader provides the first activity that must be done, and the child gives their choice of the second activity. For example, "My choice is to kick the ball to the wall five times. Your choice is to squeeze the gator ball."

With some students, the leader may need to offer two choices if the student's first choice would be to leave the physical education class, activity, or game. A choice of a certain colored ball or Hula-Hoop can be the choice for an unmotivated student. If a student is really enjoying the class, they will have their favorite activity or game chosen very quickly. Let the child decide what they would like to do with the piece of equipment. The student could either throw or kick a ball or squish or roll the ball.

First This, Then That

A similar strategy to increase motivation and alleviate anxiety about what is next uses the phrase "First this, then that." The lesson activity is the first activity, "First this," and either a continuation of the content or a preferred activity is the "Then that." The following are some examples: "First we will play games in the gym and then we will go back to the classroom." "Today we are going to play with Hula-Hoops. First we are going to run around the Hula-Hoops on the floor, and then we will roll the Hula-Hoop on the floor." Another example can be used when breaking down a skill, such as kicking a ball. "First step (cueing the nondominant foot) and then kick."

Preferred Movements

Knowing the child's preferred movements can be the beginning of much more learning. Certain movements, such as rocking, spinning, running, tippy toe walking, and jumping for a child who is seeking movement, can be used to motivate a child and actually stimulate their mind to help with learning new skills or concepts. However, each child is an individual and enjoys many different ways of moving. Just observing the child's play will easily point the leader in the right direction.

Goal Setting, Token Boards, and Rewards

Children need motivation and rewards to keep them working toward their goals because keeping their attention may be difficult. Goal setting and reward systems help participants to put their best effort toward participation. Set realistic goals and expectations with each child.

Leaders may need to remind participants to maintain focus and remember the goal to be achieved throughout the activity session. Using a special interest token board and a favorite toy or object as a reward will give a visual aid and something to look forward to after the session. Using different equipment and many visual props also helps encourage participation.

Token boards and incentive charts are a reminder to students of what their goals are, and they are a measure (that students can actually see) of how close the students are to meeting the goals or being rewarded with tangibles. They are a great way to mark individual progress for the child and for the leader. These are also great tools for keeping the child motivated and on track without the other children becoming aware that they are getting different treatment.

For most children, positive reinforcement rather than removing privileges works better for motivation. This strategy keeps the environment positive and motivates the child to perform given tasks. Use tangible reinforcers (small toys, stickers, music, or favorite foods, if all else fails) and pair with adult attention (Allen et al., 2011).

Be specific with verbal reinforcement. Saying "Good" will be too vague, whereas "good jumping and landing on both feet" is much clearer (Reid et al., 2003). Develop a reward system for good attitudes and positive behaviors. Simple and immediate rewards work, such as providing nonverbal encouragement with high fives and cheering when effort is given or success is achieved.

Sense of Control

Physical activity and physical education can be environments and situations that cause anxiety and discomfort for the student on the spectrum. In order to improve the situation and give meaning and value to these activities, it is important to give a sense of control for the student. As mentioned previously, children on the spectrum crave stability and continuity, so any change in the schedule can be upsetting. Giving the student a sense of control in these somewhat unstable settings can greatly affect the outcome of the lesson. Table 3.4 provides examples of what the student can control in individual and group situations.

In looking at the table it seems much simpler and a much more controlled environment doing an activity one on one, but the leader can give one choice to the student and choose the rest. For example, the leader can give a choice of equipment and then decide length of time, space, and activity with the chosen equipment. In a physical education class it is much more difficult to have control, especially with the space and noise level, but the student can choose to use a preferred colored rubber ball and not a soccer ball if they are more comfortable with it and like to do multiple tasks with it. Also, the student can choose to spend 5 or 10 or 30 minutes (can use a countdown clock) in the class or they can choose the number of repetitions or tasks they do in the class.

Table 3.4 Aspects Under a Student's Control in Individual and Group Sessions

	INDIVIDUAL SESSION WITH AN EA	GROUP (PHYSICAL EDUCATION CLASS)
THE STUDENT CAN CONTROL	The space	The equipment
	The length of session	The level of participation with others
	The number of repetitions	The length of time in class*
	The equipment	
THE STUDENT CAN'T CONTROL	The task (EA decides)	The space
		The activity or task
		The level of noise
		The number of people in class.

*A student may choose to participate in only a portion of the lesson, such as the warm-up, or to complete a specific number of tasks.

Conclusion

As mentioned, effective teaching begins with the planning of the content, the delivery, and the learning environment. Because each child on the spectrum is a different child, one must see teaching through a different lens. Through appropriate communication, conscious consideration of the environment, and matching instructional strategies to students' strengths, children can develop physical literacy, motivation to move, self-confidence, and enhanced social skills.

I began working with a participant who didn't like to play or do any type of games in the gym. She only liked using the "big people" equipment like the cardio and weight machines in the fitness center. She wanted to be an adult and would have tantrums about not being little. She was only seven years old and did not fit in most of the machines. I decided to try using the iPad as a reward at the end of her sessions, and it worked; she would rush through all the assigned "kid" activities and then want to play various games on the iPad (Angry Birds, Smurfs, etc.). A couple of months later we received new treadmills and bikes that allowed for smartphones and tablets to be plugged into them, and this changed everything for me because she was no longer rushing through certain activities. She had never liked the treadmill because she found it boring, but now she didn't realize that she was on the treadmill for more than 60 seconds because she was able to play her game while doing the activity.

Erin Bennett

Fundamental Movement Skills

Physical activity is vital to all aspects of children's growth and development. Early childhood is the time to begin the development of active, healthy lifestyles. Children from zero to four years require 180 minutes of physical activity at any intensity per day using a variety of activities in different environments. By age five, children require 60 minutes of energetic physical activity daily, which also includes strengthening muscle and bone at least three days per week. By breathing hard and sweating a little, children will be physically active enough for healthy development.

But being physically active doesn't just magically happen. Children need assistance to develop the knowledge, skills, and attitudes that lead to continual involvement in physical activity (Canadian Society for Exercise Physiology, 2021). Benefits of physical activity during this time include the following:

- Leads to future success in skill development by helping children enjoy being active
- Teaches to move efficiently
- Improves balance and coordination
- Creates neural connections across multiple pathways
- Enhances brain function, coordination, social skills, leadership, and imagination
- Helps build strong bones, improves flexibility, develops good posture, promotes healthy body weight
- Reduces stress and improves sleep (Sport for Life, 2016)

A child on the spectrum might require different approaches to learn the skills, knowledge, and attitudes needed to become physically active. They might differ from their peers with regard to visual tracking, mental processing, attention span, joint attention, and motivation. This might be in addition to gross or fine motor abilities that are impaired or low fitness levels (i.e., cardiovascular, muscle strength and endurance, agility, and flexibility). Differences in social skills and sensory sensitivities might also contribute to some disadvantages for children on the spectrum while participating in physical activities. Trying to coordinate muscle groups, understand strategy, and engage in social communication may lead to the child feeling overwhelmed.

When working with young children on the spectrum, avoid trying to make a child be "normal." In many schools, the attitude that children on the spectrum need to be cured, fixed, tempered, or basically changed to be more acceptable as human beings is harmful to everyone. The message a child should receive is, "There is nothing wrong with you. You are just different. These are the problems you are going to face but it will get better" (Fletcher-Watson & Happe, 2019, p. 99). Teachers and educational assistants provide hope for the student and their family on the journey to physical literacy.

This first section introduces the ABCs of physical literacy for children in the early years. The ABCs provide the foundation for fundamental movement skills (FMS). FMS are the building blocks to successful integration into grade 1 and elementary school physical education, recess activities, and playground opportunities. The majority of this chapter introduces each fundamental movement skill, breaks the skill down to its basic elements, provides teaching techniques, and describes games and activities to accompany each of the skills. Although some children will require more time to achieve these skills, the goal for schools and families is to develop a foundation to support the child in the early years.

ABCs of Physical Literacy

Most children love to play. "All development—physical, emotional, social and cognitive—is inter-related. Young children's learning is not compartmentalized. Thus movement-learning experiences encompass and interface with all areas of development. . . . Movement experiences are a primary source for learning by young children" (Sanders, 2002, p. 9). The early years are important for social, physical, and emotional development needed for inclusion in recess activities, physical education class, and community activity programs.

The ABCs of physical literacy are agility, balance, coordination, and speed (see figure 4.1). These components form the foundation of all movement and fundamental movement and sports skills. Movement such as running, hopping, climbing, balancing, and jumping should be part of their physical activities. With increased ability to control and coordinate movements, skill development in the areas of throwing, kicking, skating, catching, and biking can be introduced and practiced.

FIGURE 4.1 The ABCs of physical literacy.

Teaching Fundamental Movement Skills

When teaching the ABCs and fundamental movement skills, plan for an optimal and safe learning environment where children can move and explore. For children with less strength, adapt by lowering targets, reducing distances to targets, and using smaller and lighter equipment. At this age, each child needs their own equipment (e.g., a ball to play with) and many practice opportunities (Sanders, 2002). Be consistent when getting out and putting away equipment (e.g., balls are stored in individual containers and marked with a picture or symbol). Use a sticker chart as a reward system.

When teaching, the leader's observation point is important for instruction and feedback. Leaders can't help what they can't see in the movement skill. Leaders must stand where they can see and be safe.

When providing instruction and feedback, be at the level of the child. Keep instruction short and simple. Give only one instruction to change at a time with young children. Be direct and tell the child what needs to be done, not what they did wrong. The leader must make sure that the child understands what to do by asking the child what they are going to do on their next attempt. Say "Tell me what you are going to do . . . ." Listen to what they tell you. Pay attention. If you don't understand, ask for clarification. Remember that your body language says more about your attitude than your words.

Children also need a variety of experiences leading to more mature fundamental movement patterns. The physical literacy goal is to learn the ABCs and fundamental movements and link them together into play (*Long Term Development*, 2022). Children need to practice skills of running, skipping, galloping, balancing, hopping, jumping, throwing, striking, and catching. Each movement skill has a readiness-to-learn time phase, and many skills develop during the early years. Development of each of these skills is a lengthy process occurring over time using activities that include basic locomotor and object control skills, activities that develop balance and stimulate the sensorimotor system, cardiovascular endurance activities, whole body movements, and dance for parallel body part identification.

Early exposure to skills will more likely result in an active life in recreational and sporting activities. By exposing a child on the spectrum to fundamental movement skills early in life, the chance of that individual continuing to participate in recreational activities throughout their entire life is increased. Learning locomotor, object control, and body control skills creates a well-rounded and physically literate individual.

As mentioned, the next section will break down select fundamental movement skills into their basic elements, with examples of teaching techniques and games to be used in creating a motivating learning environment. Each fundamental movement skill can be described as developing in three stages: emerging (stage 1), developing (stage 2), and mature (stage 3) (*NCCP Fundamental Movement Skills*, 2018). *Emerging* refers to the pattern that occurs when a person first begins to move. Children in the early years typically demonstrate emerging patterns. *Developing* refers to the pattern where the central elements of the skill are known but inconsistently performed. *Mature* refers to a consistent and accurate pattern of the skill. Mature patterns are required for the development of sport skills. This chapter's activities are meant to help children move from an emerging to a developing pattern. Participation in games and sports (the focus of chapter 5) helps children move from developing to mature patterns. The instructions in this chapter include illustrations of the movement, as well as key instructions for execution of the skill (represented by a key icon ✑) and feedback and corrections to watch for to encourage the transition from emerging to developing patterns (represented by an eyeglasses icon ⊘⊘).

When teaching the ABCs and fundamental movement skills, there are three key body principles.

1. Use all the body parts (joints) that can be used.
2. Use the body parts through as great a range of motion as is naturally possible.
3. Use the parts (joints) in order. For example, for kicking, the order is trunk, hip, knee, ankle (NCCP Fundamental Movement Skills, 2018, p. 24).

Movement is created in phases. The phases are generally the same for all skills.

- Preparation: The backswing
- Force production: The swing forward toward an object
- Critical instant: Moment of release, or the connection with the object
- Follow through: Continued movement in the direction that one wants the "force" to go (NCCP Fundamental Movement Skills, 2018, p.24).

The four movement phases are applied to a mature throwing pattern in figure 4.2. In the preparation phase, the throwing arm is drawn back. In the force production phase, the throwing arm is raised to face the target direction, and the muscles from the trunk, shoulder, arm, and wrist work together in order to create the force on the ball. At the critical instant, the ball is released. In the follow-through phase, the body parts continue to move in the target direction.

Mature throw (Stage 3)

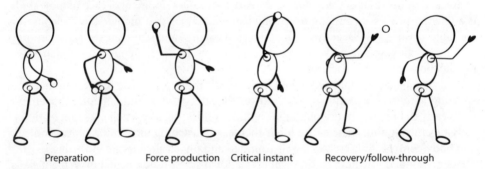

| Preparation | Force production | Critical instant | Recovery/follow-through |

FIGURE 4.2 The four movement phases applied to a mature throwing pattern.
Adapted from NCCP, "Fundamental Movement Skills," (Coaching Association of Canada, 2018), 22.

Teaching the three key body principles and applying the principles to movement phases provide the opportunity for children to learn the ABCs and sets a foundation for fundamental movement skills. The following sections define the ABCs, provide specific instructions, and describe fun games for children.

ABCs: Agility, Balance, Coordination, and Speed

The ABCs form the foundation of fundamental movement skills. Each will be defined, and some teaching principles and game descriptions are provided.

Agility

Agility is the ability to put different movement skills together, smoothly and rapidly. Agility includes stopping, changing direction, moving forward, backward, and sideways. Children will need instruction and practice time to become aware of where all their body parts are at all times (arms, legs). Give them the following guidelines:

- Lean in the direction of travel to start quickly.
- Lean in the opposite direction of travel to stop quickly.
- Land and stay low for greater stability.
- Bend knees to absorb the force of landing over as great an area as possible.

Balance

Balance is the ability to maintain a controlled body position while it moves in space. Balance is attained when the center of gravity is over the base of support. There are equal amounts of weight on all sides of the center of gravity. The lower the center of gravity, the easier it is to balance. The base includes all the parts of the body in contact with the floor and all the space between the contact points. The bigger or wider the base, the easier to balance. The stiffer the body, the easier to balance. Arm action can help maintain dynamic balance. Dynamic balance is easier when you are moving because you are constantly adjusting the base of support to bring it under the center of gravity.

Adapted from Sport for Life, *Developing Physical Literacy: A Guide for Parents of Children Ages 0-12*, (Vancouver: Canadian Sport Centres, 2016). https://sportforlife.ca/wp-content/uploads/2016/12/DPL_ENG_Feb29.indd_.pdf.

Coordination and Speed

Coordination is controlling all of one's body parts while doing different activities. It is making and maintaining connections between the brain and the muscles that control movement. Speed refers to how quickly a person can travel a specific distance. The more speed a person has, the quicker the person can move to a specific location. The following sections introduce instruction and games to develop the ABCs.

Be a T

Students try to make a T shape with their bodies to learn how to balance and help in practicing to keep balance. Ask students to move across the space holding their T shape following lines on the floor or standing on objects such as a stability pod or foam balance beam.

Equipment

- Lines or tape on floor
- Stability equipment, such as Both Sides Up (BOSU) balance trainer or another type of balance training equipment
- Stability pods
- Foam balance beams

Instructions

- Lines on a gym floor can be used for a simplified version of this activity.
- The individual is instructed to move across the room either on the lines or on the equipment.
- Use the verbal and visual cues in order to increase stability for the individual.

Cues

- Verbal: "Arms like a T"
- Visual: Hold arms out like the letter *T*

Modifications

- To increase the difficulty and balance, increase the speed of the movement across the room. Stability equipment, such as BOSUs, stability pods, or foam balance beams, can also be included to increase the level of difficulty.

Do This Balance

Static balance involves the maintenance of a desired pose in a stationary position. The center of gravity needs to be over the individual's base of support to ensure greater balance. This game allows the participant to practice the skill of copying as well as practicing their balance. The instructor verbally cues the participant to do various dynamic balance positions.

Equipment

- Polyspots

Instructions

- Polyspots are spread out in the playing space.
- The activity begins with both instructor and participant facing each other and then progressing to more complicated movements.
- Instruct the individual to stand on one foot on the polyspot.
- Time needs to be given to the participant to process what is being asked of them.
- The instructor can stand for a count of 5 to 10 seconds and increase as ability grows.

Cues

- Verbal: "Hold" or "Hold for [number of seconds]"
- Visual: Hands out like the letter *T*

Modifications

- To increase stability, have the individual extend their arms out in a T position.
- The individual can try to put one hand on a polyspot and one foot on a polyspot and balance in a more difficult position.

Number Balances

This activity allows the participant to explore balance and body awareness in the same activity.

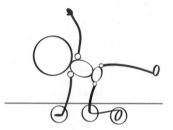

Instructions

- The instructor tells the participant a number, which is the number of body parts that the participant is able to use for balance.

Modifications

- Begin with a simple number, such as two (the participant can then stand on two feet) and add on as the participant becomes more comfortable with the activity.

Run and Stop

This warm-up game is a great way to use the verbal and visual cues of STOP and GO while moving freely around the space.

Equipment

- One can use pylons to set a boundary, but this is not necessary because it can become a distraction as well.

Instructions

- Have the group move freely around an area.
- Begin the game by having students move around, and then cue "stop" quickly to throw them off balance a bit more.
- Use faster transitions between "go" and "stop" to increase difficulty.

Cues

- Introduce and review the cues of "go" (fingers point ahead) and STOP (hands in reverse T position).

Follow the Leader

This warm-up game allows the introduction of various locomotor skills led by the instructor and can be used as a creative outlet by the students to lead the group on their own. This is a good opportunity for learning and practicing turn taking as well.

Equipment

- Polyspots

Instructions

- Students play follow the leader while stepping on lines or polyspots.
- Skip over certain colors or spaces in order to increase difficulty. Line tag requires all participants to move only on lines (Boulton, n.d.).

Twister

Twisting is a type of movement that requires the body to move through space around its own axis. This activity encourages twisting side to side while touching a ball to the floor.

Equipment

- Foam ball
- Medicine ball

Instructions

- The individual sits on the floor with their feet extended in front of them.
- The instructor gives the individual a ball (or medicine ball for stronger individuals).
- The individual is then instructed to twist their upper body to one side and touch the ball down to the floor beside them.
- Next, the individual will twist their upper body to the other side and touch the ball down to the floor beside them.
- The instructor gives the verbal cue to "touch the floor" with the ball.

Cues

- Verbal: "Twisting" or "side to side"

Modifications

The individual can do the exercise standing up with their back against a wall. The individual holds the ball in their hands and twists their upper body side to side and touches the ball to the wall on each twist.

Ribbon Twirling or Bubbles

This activity allows the student to move freely and creatively with a bubble wand or ribbon stick while being cued to move in various directions (up, down, sideways). This fun activity can be used on a rainy or snowy day to imitate the weather outside.

Instructions

- The participant is given a rhythmic gymnastics ribbon or craft ribbon.
- The participant is instructed to move the ribbon fast and slow using the twisting motion practiced earlier.

Modifications

- This activity can also use blowing bubbles instead of a ribbon in warming weather outdoors.

Locomotor Skills

Locomotor skills are movements that transport an individual through space from one place to another. In preparation for school, children need to learn to move up and down stairs with alternating feet. The locomotor skills of running, hopping, galloping, and jumping are presented in the next section.

Stopping and changing direction safely should be emphasized throughout these lessons. One of the locomotor areas that children should master for school is alternating feet while traveling up and down stairs. Here are some hints to teach alternating feet on stairs.

Step 1: Place markers (dots or tape) or polyspots on the floor in a line and practice stepping with alternating feet on the spots.

Step 2: Place the markers on the steps and review feet taking turns walking up the stairs. Emphasize not taking two steps per step. Practice going up the stairs.

Step 3: Practice going down the stairs. Ideally the student can hold onto something like a railing in order to keep their balance. This step may require more practice.

Step 4: Put both stepping up and down together.

Step 5: Take the markers away and cue the feet taking turns up and down the stairs.

Teaching a child to go down the stairs may be more difficult than going up the stairs because a child may feel extremely uncomfortable with how their body is moving and may feel unsafe, even when one physically holds them. Use full physical prompts to move feet alternating down the stairs. The child needs to actually feel how their body moves through a specific action in order to get more comfortable with it. Children need to feel secure and safe while doing it, and reassured that their leader can be trusted to keep them safe. Don't force the child, but take the opportunity to work through the initial stages of this new action so they will get more comfortable with how their body feels performing it. Once they are feeling more stable with the action, one can start getting creative with other ways of helping the child do the same movement. This could start with something simple and then move into some type of game.

Running

Running is a natural extension of walking with a flight phase. It can be characterized by an alternate support phase, flight phase, and recovery phase. Running and chasing are difficult for some individuals. This may be a skill that needs to be practiced. Figure 4.3 shows a breakdown of the phases of the run.

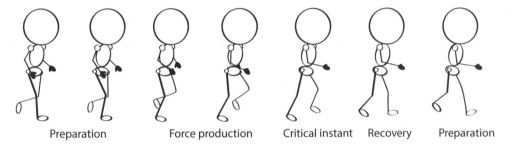

| Preparation | Force production | Critical instant | Recovery | Preparation |

FIGURE 4.3 Phases of the run.

Adapted by permission from NCCP, "Fundamental Movement Skills," *Community Leader Workshop–Coach Workbook,* (Coaching Association of Canada: 2018), 28.

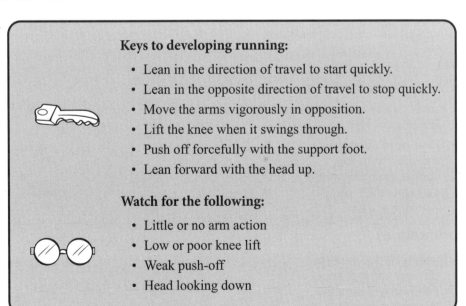

Keys to developing running:

- Lean in the direction of travel to start quickly.
- Lean in the opposite direction of travel to stop quickly.
- Move the arms vigorously in opposition.
- Lift the knee when it swings through.
- Push off forcefully with the support foot.
- Lean forward with the head up.

Watch for the following:

- Little or no arm action
- Low or poor knee lift
- Weak push-off
- Head looking down

Adapted by permission from NCCP, "Fundamental Movement Skills," *Community Leader Workshop–Coach Workbook,* (Coaching Association of Canada: 2018), 28.

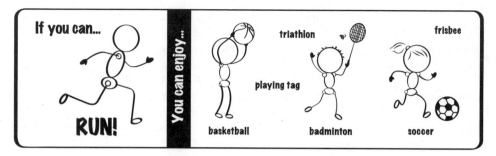

Adapted from Sport for Life, *Deveioping Physical Literacy: A Guide for Parents of Children Ages 0-12*, (Vancouver: Canadian Sport Centres, 2016). https://sportforlife.ca/wp-content/uploads/2016/12/DPL_ENG_Feb29.indd_.pdf.

This game encourages students to run and chase their rocket while practicing correct running technique.

Equipment

- Foam rockets (to initiate chasing)
- Ball, beanbag, or pylons

Instructions

- Begin by walking, then cue to go faster.
- Individual can be cued to run to certain predetermined objects in the room.
- Foam rockets can be used to initiate chasing by having the individual launch the rocket and then go pick it up.
- Polyspots can be used in a row and having the individual step on the mats quickly.

Cues

- Verbal: "Run" or "chase"
- Instructor can also cue the individual to "touch" certain objects in the room by running to them.
- Visual: object that the individual runs to, something that is motivating for the individual, such as a ball.

Modifications

- Increase or decrease the distance the individual needs to run, depending on the mobility level of the individual.

The game of tag is the basis of most games and sports taught in schools. Teaching tag to individuals on the spectrum can prove to be challenging because they may not be comfortable touching other people continuously in a physical activity setting. Also some of the students may not be allowed to touch other students if they tend to have aggressive behaviors.

Instructions

- Introduce the idea of tag by having the students walk and touch or tag (emphasizing gentle hands) various colored items or locations in the room or gym.
- The instructor calls out 5 to 10 different items or areas in the room, and the students will all touch that item or location at the same time to get used to being closer together.
- One can increase the speed of the game or the number of locations. Locations or items, such as doors, floor, nets, walls, and benches can all be used.

Equipment

- No equipment. Just ensure that the locations to be touched are safe and clean for all students.

Modifications

- To progress, have one student wear a pinny. Reinforce the color of the pinny and the use of gentle hands when touching the pinny on the person.
- Have students take turns trying to individually tag the person with the pinny on. Begin with walking to the person trying to tag them and then increase speed when students begin grasping the concept of chasing and being chased.
- Once this idea is understood, add in more pinnies on more students so that there are more opportunities to tag one another.

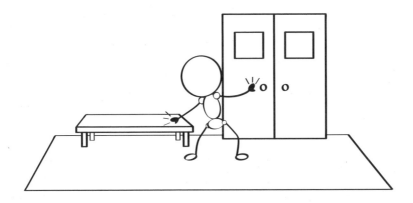

Ship to Shore (Ball to Pylon)

This is a well-known game where the students move from one area to another area repeatedly as the instructor names the area to where the students should move. This game can be a fun and creative way to warm up and be silly. Cues such as "walk the plank," "captain's coming!" and "wash the deck" can be added (Ultimate Camp Resource, n.d.).

Equipment
- Use objects that are familiar and motivating for the participant.

Instructions
- Two objects are set a certain distance apart.
- The distance needs to be appropriate for the participant.
- Instructor demonstrates running to object 1, then stops.
- The instructor then runs to object 2, then stops.

Cues
- Cue the participant to run to object 1, then stop.
- Then cue the participant to run to object 2, then stop. Continue this cycle until it becomes fluid.

Modifications
- If the participant has a greater understanding of the game, the instructor can play ship to shore. The instructor indicates where the "ship" is located and where the "shore" is.
- Instruct the participant to run to either location.
- The instructor can then add in different locomotor skills, such as hopping or rolling between locations.
- These can be cued with the locomotor skill name or cues, such as "seagull walk" or "seaweed roll" if appropriate.

Jumping

Jumping projects a person into the air by force generated in one or both legs. The individual lands on one or both feet. Figure 4.4 shows emerging (*a*), developing (*b*), and mature (*c*) patterns of jumping as jumpers improve their execution of the preparation, force production, critical instant, and recovery phases.

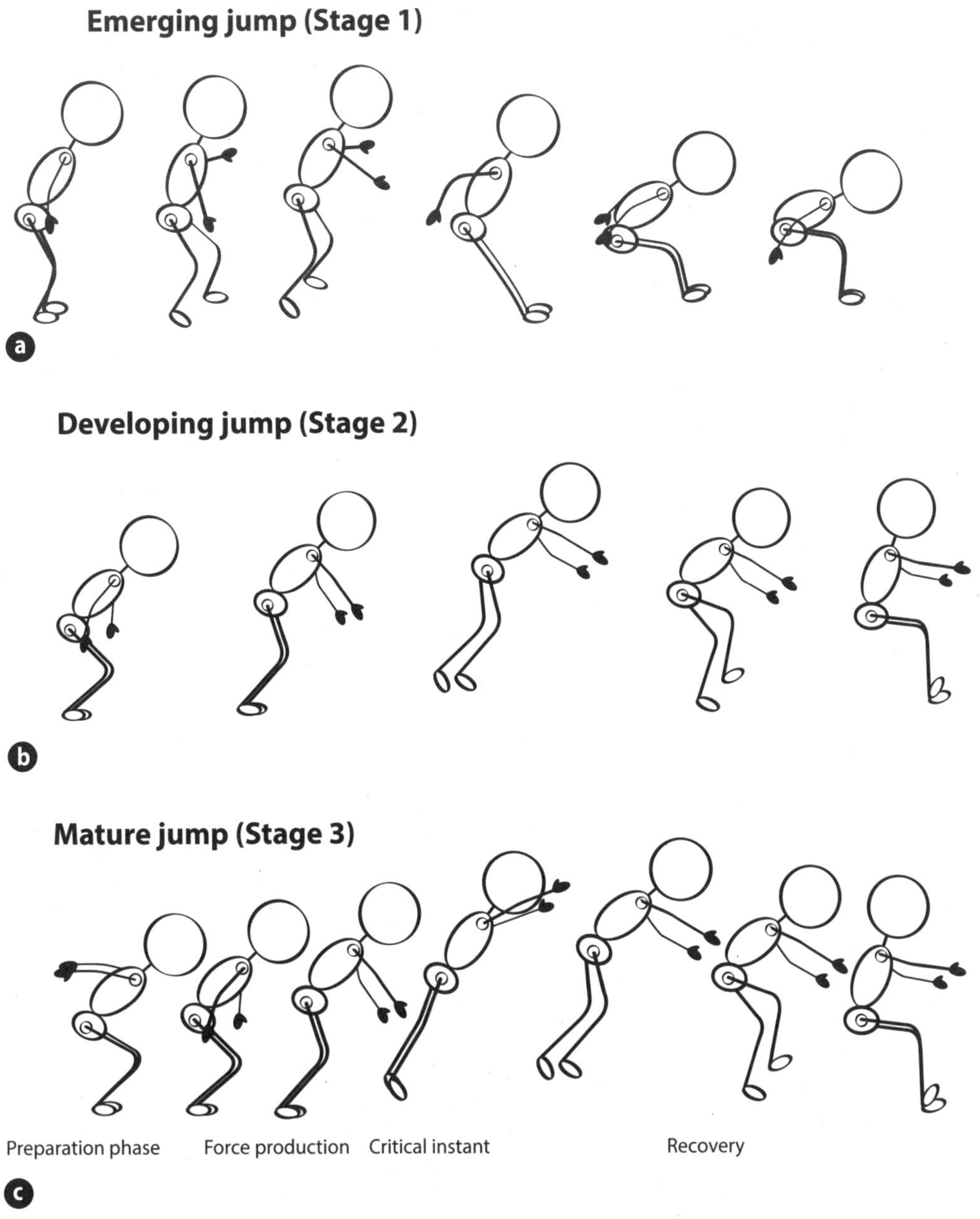

Emerging jump (Stage 1)

Developing jump (Stage 2)

Mature jump (Stage 3)

Preparation phase   Force production   Critical instant   Recovery

FIGURE 4.4 Growth progression for jumping: emerging (*a*), developing (*b*), and mature (*c*) patterns.

Adapted by permission from NCCP, "Fundamental Movement Skills," *Community Leader Workshop–Coach Workbook,* (Coaching Association of Canada: 2018), 32.

Keys to a developing jump:

- Bend knees
- Swing arms forward and at the same time
- Push off both legs
- Lean forward to take off

Watch for these in the emerging jump:

- Little use of the arms or not together
- Weak push-off or using only one leg

Adapted by permission from NCCP, "Fundamental Movement Skills," *Community Leader Workshop–Coach Workbook,* (Coaching Association of Canada: 2018), 32.

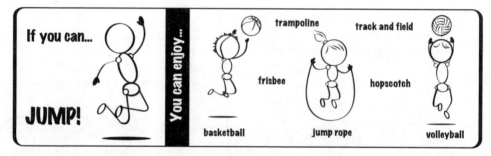

Adapted from Sport for Life, *Developing Physical Literacy: A Guide for Parents of Children Ages 0-12*, (Vancouver: Canadian Sport Centres, 2016). https://sportforlife.ca/wp-content/uploads/2016/12/DPL_ENG_Feb29.indd_.pdf.

Jumping (Two Feet) Skill Practice

Equipment

- Sticky mats or beanbags
- Mini trampoline
- Bubble Wrap can be placed on the ground for motivation.

Instructions

- Bend knees.
- Cue "swing arms."
- Cue "jump."
- Instructor may hold the individual under the arms and help lift when cueing "jump."
- If individual is able to jump independently then place a sticky mat or beanbags or a marking on the floor and have the individual jump up and down in place. This is a vertical jump.
- Emphasize landing by demonstrating straight landing arms, hands out.
- Once that is mastered, you can place another sticky mat or beanbags a few footsteps in front of the other mat and cue the individual to jump to that sticky mat (long jump). One can use a different-colored mat than the one that the individual is standing on to jump to. An example is cue "jump to red." This is a horizontal jump.
- Mini trampolines are motivating as well.

Cues

- Verbal: "Bend your knees," "swing your arms, back, front," "jump"
- Visual: Sticky mats for landing

Modifications

- Instructors can also have individuals jump down from a short step or ledge.
- This may help with momentum.

Leapfrog

This activity allows the student to practice jumping from two feet to two feet in a fun way. Increasing or decreasing the distance between polyspots can increase or decrease the challenge of this skill.

Equipment

- Polyspots

Instructions

- Polyspots are set up in a row (short or long depending on ability level).
- Instructor can curve the row to increase the difficulty.
- The participant practices taking off from two feet from one polyspot and landing with two feet on a different polyspot.

Modifications

- Jumping from a distance can also be practiced using this game.
- Polyspots are set up farther apart to increase the distance required to jump.

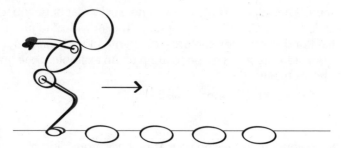

Hopping

This is a form of jumping where one foot is used to project the individual into space while landing on the same foot (see figure 4.5). Most individuals will perform better on a preferred foot. This skill is more difficult than the two-footed jump.

Preparation   Force production   Critical instant   Recovery/follow-through   Preparation

FIGURE 4.5   Phases of the hop.

Adapted by permission from NCCP, "Fundamental Movement Skills," *Community Leader Workshop–Reference Material Version 1.0*, (Coaching Association of Canada: 2009), 57.

Hopping (One Foot) Skill Practice

Equipment

- Sticky mats or beanbags
- Mini trampoline

Instructions

- Bend knees.
- Cue "swing arms."
- Cue "hop."
- Instructor may hold the individual under the arms and help lift when
- cueing "hop."
- If individual is able to hop independently, then place a sticky mat or beanbags or a marking on the floor and have the individual hop up and down in place. This is a vertical hop.
- Emphasize landing by demonstrating straight landing arms, hands out.
- Once that is mastered, you can place another sticky mat or beanbags a few footsteps in front of the other mat and cue the individual to hop to that sticky mat (long hop). One can use a different-colored mat than the one that the individual is standing on to hop to. An example is cue "hop to red." This is a horizontal hop.
- Mini trampolines are motivating as well.

Cues

- Verbal: "Bend," "hop"

Modifications

- Instructors may need to physically hold the nonpreferred leg up and cue the individual to hop. This works best on a trampoline.

Hopping Leapfrog

This activity allows the student to practice hopping in a fun way by setting up the polyspots in various ways that can increase or decrease the challenge of this skill.

Equipment

- Polyspots

Instructions

- Polyspots can be lined up in a row.
- The participant can hop from poly-spot to polyspot.

Modifications

- Line up a row of different-colored polyspots and call out a color for the partici-pant to hop on and hop off.

Hop On

This activity introduces the idea of jumping or hopping up or down onto an object. For example, hopping up the stairs or jumping off a small ledge (when safe to do so).

Equipment

- Small trampoline or BOSU

Instructions

- Instructor uses a small trampoline or BOSU.
- Participant can begin by jumping on the equipment.

Cues

- Instructor verbally cues the participant to "jump on two legs."
- Once the participant succeeds with this activity, the instructor cues the partici-pant to "hop on one leg."
- The participant may need to be physically prompted by the instructor by either a light tap on the leg or physically holding one of the participant's legs up.

Rolling

Rolling is rotating the body around one of its axes.

Rolling (Log Rolls) Skill Practice

Equipment

- Mat
- Triangle mat (optional—increases momentum, but instructor may have some resistance from individual due to the height)

Instructions

- Lay on back on the ground.
- Place palms together, hands straight overhead ("Like a pencil").
- Keep feet together.
- Roll over onto stomach, then back onto back continuously.
- Instructor may need to provide assistance in moving.

Cues

- Verbal: "Roll over," "hands together," "feet together."
- Visual: Sticky mats on floor, have individual put their stomach on mat then roll over onto their back onto another sticky mat. Vary the colors as needed for cueing.

Modifications

- Instructor can give small pressure squeezes on shoulders or back as motivation each time individual rolls over.

Log Rollover

This activity allows the participant to practice log rolls while also feeling the various textures under them. This creates a motivating activity.

Equipment

- Materials such as Bubble Wrap, cardboard, brown paper, or gymnastic mats.

Instructions

- Lay different materials in a row on the floor.
- The instructor tells the participant to roll over each item in the row.
- Participants tend to enjoying playing with various fabrics and textures.

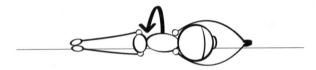

Galloping

Galloping is a forward step followed by a leap onto the trailing foot (see figure 4.6). The same leg always leads, and the skill is performed in a front-facing position.

FIGURE 4.6   Phases of the gallop.

Adapted by permission from NCCP, "Fundamental Movement Skills," *Community Leader Workshop–Reference Material Version 1.0,* (Coaching Association of Canada: 2009), 57.

Galloping Skill Practice

Equipment

- Stickers (popular characters, colors, cars, trains, animals, etc.)
- Sticky mats

Instructions

- Place sticker onto lead foot. Step lead foot onto a sticky mat and then back to the floor. Repeat until skill is comprehended.
- Add on to movement by bringing the back foot together onto the sticky mat with the lead foot.
- Then cue for the lead foot to step forward onto another sticky mat and bring the back foot up again.
- Repeat with 5 to 10 sticky mats in a row until skill is maintainable with minimal prompting.
- Remove sticky mats when appropriate. Repeat until movement is fluid and continuous.

Cues

- Verbal: "Gallop"
- Visual: Stickers, pylons for space marking

Modifications

- The instructor can use stickers that are motivating to the individual. For example the lead foot could have a sticker of a cat, and the back foot can have a sticker of a dog. The instructor will tell the individual that the dog will chase the cat but that the cat will always get away, meaning that the lead foot will always be the same for the whole movement.
- Sliding is a gallop performed in a sideways motion. It can be performed by turning the torso to a wall and is instructed in the same manner.

Stop and Go

This activity is a good warm-up game where various locomotor skills can be practiced while also following the verbal and visual instruction of "stop" and "go".

Instructions

- The participant is instructed to practice a variety of locomotor skills, such as running, walking, and skipping.
- The instructor will state a locomotor skill and say, "Go."
- The participant moves around the room doing the locomotor skill until the instructor says, "Stop."

Cues

- The instructor can use hand signals to visually cue as well.

Modifications

- Galloping and listening skills can be practiced during this game.
- Direction changes can also be added in to increase the difficulty.

Skipping

When skipping, the forward step is followed by a hop on the same foot. The leading foot alternates between left and right (see figure 4.7). This is a difficult motor pattern.

FIGURE 4.7   Phases of the skip.

Adapted by permission from NCCP, "Fundamental Movement Skills," *Community Leader Workshop–Reference Material Version 1.0,* (Coaching Association of Canada: 2009), 57.

Skipping Skill Practice

Equipment
- Sticky mats (optional)
- Beanbags (optional)
- Tape (optional)

Instructions
- Lay out a straight row of sticky mats, beanbags, or tape on the floor.
- Practice marching, with high knees, emphasizing "feet taking turns."
- The individual must only step on the sticky mats, beanbags, or tape.
- Once the foot pattern is developed and performed consistently, then add in alternating arms.
- Practice this movement until it becomes continuous.
- Add in a hop after each step. Spread the sticky mats, beanbags, or tape farther apart to increase the horizontal movement of the skill.
- Practice this movement until it is continuous and fluid.

Cues
- Verbal: "Feet taking turns," "big knees," "swing arms"
- Rhythmic: hop step left hop step right hop step left
- Visual: sticky mats, beanbags, or tape

Hula-Hoop Skipping

This activity allows a more advanced skipping technique to be practiced with the visual guide of Hula-Hoops lined up on the floor or ground.

Instructions

- Hula-Hoops are set up tightly side by side in a straight line.
- The participant is instructed to take one step into the first hoop and then continue the skipping motion throughout all of the hoops.

Cues

- The instructor can emphasize the height of the jumping portion of the skipping action.

Modifications

- If skipping is difficult for the participant the instructor can emphasize a slower pace so that the individual does not trip on the hoops.
- Adding more hoops can increase the difficulty of the activity.

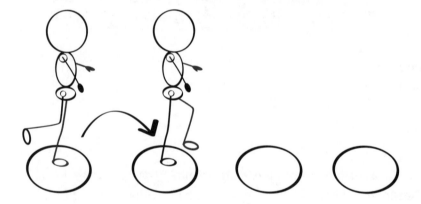

Additional games for locomotor skills can be developed by allowing the students to choose a movement pattern that they are comfortable with. It can be as simple as walking or running or as complex as skipping or hopping. Use cues such as "up," "down," "middle," "fast," "slow" in order to increase difficulty.

Sending and Receiving Skills

The fundamental movement skills of sending involve projecting an object away from the body. Sending skills will include throwing, kicking, and striking. Receiving skills involve stopping, securing, or impeding a moving object with the body, body parts, or a piece of equipment. Receiving skills included here are catching, blocking, and tackling.

Object manipulation skills (sending and receiving) involve equipment. When adapting an activity for a child, consider how to make the skill easier or harder based on these characteristics. Refer to chapter 2, table 2.4, Equipment Variability. Consider the movement characteristics of the child and the nature of the skill to determine how to adapt using equipment.

Sending

Sending skills, also called propulsion skills, enable children to enjoy many physical activities. Throwing, kicking, and striking are the most important sending skills to learn during early childhood.

Throwing

Throwing is propelling an object through the air by force generated by the arm and hand. Many physical activities involve throwing. With instruction and practice, students can move from an emerging pattern of throwing (stage 1) to a developing pattern (stage 2) to a mature pattern (stage 3). Figure 4.8 shows emerging (*a*), developing (*b*), and mature (*c*) patterns of throwing as throwers improve their execution of the preparation, force production, critical instant, and recovery or follow-through phases.

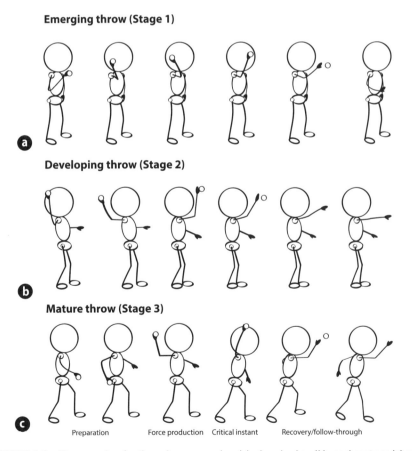

FIGURE 4.8   Progression for throwing: emerging (*a*), developing (*b*), and mature (*c*) patterns.

Adapted by permission from NCCP, "Fundamental Movement Skills," *Community Leader Workshop–Coach Workbook,* (Coaching Association of Canada: 2018), 22.

The keys to developing throwing:

- Arm is up and to the side.
- Use the shoulder, elbow, and wrist in order.
- Body points in the direction the ball will go.
- Shift body weight from back to front.

Watch for these in the emerging throw:

- Throw is only from the elbow.
- Body motion is limited.

Adapted by permission from NCCP, "Fundamental Movement Skills," *Community Leader Workshop–Coach Workbook,* (Coaching Association of Canada: 2018), 22.

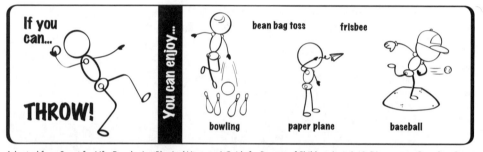

Adapted from Sport for Life, *Developing Physical Literacy: A Guide for Parents of Children Ages 0-12,* (Vancouver: Canadian Sport Centres, 2016). https://sportforlife.ca/wp-content/uploads/2016/12/DPL_ENG_Feb29.indd_.pdf.

Overhand Throwing Skill Practice

Equipment

- Beanbags
- Small ball (easier to grasp)
- Rubber chicken (allows for greater success in overhand throwing due to weight of the object)

Instructions

- Begin by cueing the individual to give the instructor a high five with their dominant hand.
- Make sure the instructor's hand is up high.
- Practice doing high fives until the skill is mastered.
- Give the individual a beanbag in the dominant hand.
- Instruct the individual to give a high five with the beanbag.
- Repeat until the skill is mastered.

- The instructor will slowly start to bring their hand (the one receiving the high fives) closer to themselves so that the individual must reach farther and farther to complete the task.
- Instruct the individual to begin to throw. This may occur naturally due to the instructor moving their hand away. Once this skill is mastered, a ball can replace the beanbag.
- Use the verbal cue of "big throw" to distinguish overhand throwing from underhand throwing.

Cues

- Verbal: "Step and throw," "big throw," or "high five throw," and "elbow up"
- Rhythmic: Step, elbow up, and throw
- Visual: Sticky mats for stepping, tape or marker on the wall to provide a target to which to throw

Beanbag Overhand Throw to Hoop

This activity practices overhand throwing by using a Hula-Hoop (or multiple hoops) as a target. Hoops can be on the ground or held at various heights by the instructor.

Equipment

- Various colored Hula-Hoops
- Beanbags

Instructions

- Two to four Hula-Hoops (of various colors) are lined up in a row.
- The instructor demonstrates throwing a beanbag (overhand) into a hoop.
- The participant is not allowed to pass a certain line on the floor.
- The skill of stepping in opposition is emphasized.
- The participant will try to get the beanbag into each Hula-Hoop.

Cues

- Verbal: "High five," "elbow up," "throw"

Modifications

- Use a rubber chicken because it allows for throwing action due to the added weight of the item.

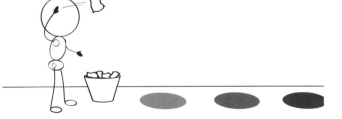

Beanbag Underhand Throw to Hoop

This activity practices underhand throwing by using a Hula-Hoop (or multiple hoops) as a target. Hoops can be on the ground or held at various heights by the instructor.

Equipment

- Various colored Hula-Hoops
- Beanbags

Instructions

- Begin by cueing the individual to give the instructor a low five with their dominant hand.
- Make sure the instructor's hand is turned prone (fingers facing down). The individual will give the instructor a low five.
- Practice doing low fives until the skill is mastered.
- Give the individual a beanbag in the dominant hand.
- Instruct the individual to give a low five with the beanbag.
- Repeat until the skill is mastered.
- The instructor will slowly start to bring their hand (the one receiving the low fives) closer to themselves so that the individual must reach farther and farther to complete the task.
- Instruct the individual to begin to throw. This may occur naturally due to the instructor moving their hand away. Once this skill is mastered, a ball can replace the beanbag.
- Use the verbal cue of "little throw" to distinguish underhand throwing from overhand throwing.

Cues

- Verbal: "Low-five," "throw"

Modifications

- In order to determine dominance, ask the individual to use the hand that they eat with or that they write their name with.

Circle Bowling

This game allows a group to practice their bowling skills all together with the goal of knocking over all the pins as quickly as possible. Team building and social interaction are part of the game.

Equipment

- Bowling pins

Instructions

- Set up bowling pins in a circular pattern.
- If there is a circle drawn on the gym floor put all the bowling pins inside the circle for more structure.
- The participant is allowed to roll or underhand throw a ball toward the group of bowling pins.
- The participant is allowed to move around the outside of the circle freely. Stepping in opposition is encouraged before the ball is thrown.

Cues

- Verbal: "Low-five," "throw"

Modifications

- This game can be played individually or with a group.
- In order to increase difficulty, the instructor can name a colored bowling pin that is to be hit by the participant.
- To decrease the level of difficulty only use a small number of bowling pins.

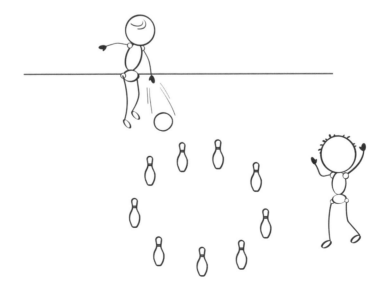

Kicking

The fundamental movement skill of kicking requires balance and coordination. To kick, the student must balance on one leg while swinging the opposite leg. With instruction and practice, students can move from an emerging pattern (stage 1) to a developing pattern (stage 2) and then to a mature pattern (stage 3). Figure 4.9 shows emerging (*a*), developing (*b*), and mature (*c*) patterns of kicking as kickers improve their execution of the preparation, force production, critical instant, and follow-through phases.

Emerging kick (Stage 1)

Developing kick (Stage 2)

Mature kick (Stage 3)

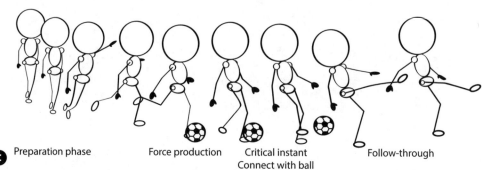

Preparation phase   Force production   Critical instant   Follow-through
Connect with ball

FIGURE 4.9 Growth progression for kicking: emerging (*a*), developing (*b*), and mature (*c*) patterns.

Adapted by permission from NCCP, "Fundamental Movement Skills," *Community Leader Workshop–Coach Workbook*, (Coaching Association of Canada: 2018), 66.

The keys to developing kicking:
- Contact ball with toe or laces.
- Follow through with leg pointing straight ahead.
- Use straight-on approach.
- Bend knee back.

Watch for these in the emerging kick:
- Kicker stands still
- No backswing from kicking hip
- Limited kicking knee bend
- Erratic arm action
- No follow-through

Adapted by permission from NCCP, "Fundamental Movement Skills," *Community Leader Workshop–Coach Workbook,* (Coaching Association of Canada: 2018), 36.

Adapted from Sport for Life, *Developing Physical Literacy: A Guide for Parents of Children Ages 0-12,* (Vancouver: Canadian Sport Centres, 2016). https://sportforlife.ca/wp-content/uploads/2016/12/DPL_ENG_Feb29.indd_.pdf.

Kicking Skill Practice

Equipment

- An appropriately sized ball for the size of the individual in order to have success with stopping the ball.

Instructions

- Have the individual stand with their nondominant foot on a sticky mat.
- Place a beanbag or ball in front of the individual's dominant foot.
- Instruct the individual to kick the ball.
- Practice until the skill is mastered with little assistance or prompts.
- To stop the ball, cue the individual to "squish" the ball with their foot. This means to step down on the ball in order to stop the ball.
- Practice the skill of stopping the ball until mastered.
- String the two skills together.

Cues

- Verbal: "Kick," "squish"
- Visual: Place a sticker on the dominant foot (foot that is kicking) as a visual reminder of which foot the individual is to kick with.
- Use a sticky mat to remind the individual which foot is to stay in place (support leg).

Modifications

- Practicing this skill on grass instead of on a smooth gym floor can help slow the speed of the ball.
- Advance to stopping the ball by drawing back the leg on contact (absorb the ball).

Three-Pylon Kick

This game is a fun way to practice kicking with the dominant and nondominant foot and making lots of noise in the process.

Equipment

- Three pylons

Instructions

- Three pylons are set up in a triangular pattern.
- The instructor stands at one pylon, and the participant stands at another. The instructor kicks a ball to the participant.
- The participant stops the ball with his or her foot.
- The instructor moves to a different pylon, and the participant kicks the ball back to the instructor.
- Once the instructor has the ball, the participant then moves to another pylon, and the cycle continues.

Modifications

- This game works on kicking skills as well as spatial awareness.

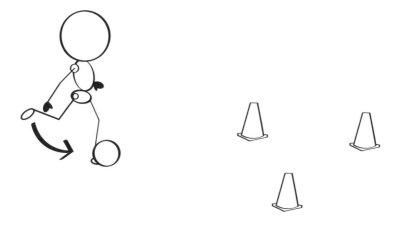

Striking

Striking typically involves an implement, such as a bat, stick, club, paddle, or racquet. The striking pattern occurs in different planes. Baseball uses a horizontal plane, whereas hockey and golf travel through a vertical plane. With instruction and practice, students can move from an emerging striking pattern (stage 1) to a developing striking pattern (stage 2) to a mature striking pattern (stage 3). Figure 4.10 shows emerging (*a*), developing (*b*), and mature (*c*) patterns of striking as strikers improve their execution of the preparation, force production, critical instant, and recovery phases.

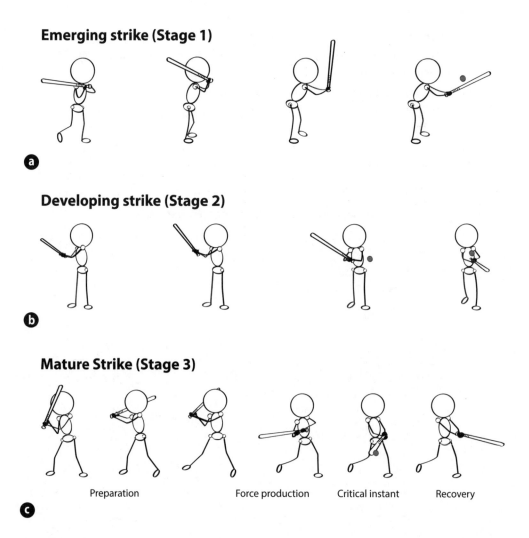

FIGURE 4.10   Growth progression for striking: emerging (*a*), developing (*b*), and mature (*c*) patterns.

Adapted by permission from NCCP, "Fundamental Movement Skills," *Community Leader Workshop–Coach Workbook,* (Coaching Association of Canada: 2018), 40.

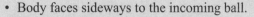

Keys to a developing striking pattern:

- Body faces sideways to the incoming ball.
- Watch the ball approach.
- Start with feet spread apart, knees bent.
- Bring arms behind head and elbows high.
- Swing forward and level.
- Contact with arms straight.
- Follow through in the direction of the swing.

Watch for these in the emerging striking pattern:

- Feet facing forward
- Body facing forward
- Vertical chopping motion rather than horizontal-level swing motion

Adapted by permission from NCCP, "Fundamental Movement Skills," *Community Leader Workshop–Coach Workbook,* (Coaching Association of Canada: 2018), 40.

Adapted from Sport for Life, *Developing Physical Literacy: A Guide for Parents of Children Ages 0-12,* (Vancouver: Canadian Sport Centres, 2016). https://sportforlife.ca/wp-content/uploads/2016/12/DPL_ENG_Feb29.indd_.pdf.

Striking (Batting) Skill Practice

Equipment

- String or rope
- Implement (bat or racquet)
- Tape
- Small ball with holes (Omni ball), badminton shuttlecock
- T-ball (optional)

Instructions

- Begin by having the individual hold the desired implement in their hand for a desired time (could be for 3 to 60 seconds).
- Cue the individual to "swing" the bat.
- Tie a small ball or balloon to the end of a string or rope that is hanging from the middle of a doorway or from the ceiling.
- Contact with the object is made with the bat. This skill is practiced until the individual is able to make consistent swings.
- A T-ball stand may be used to practice batting before attempting to strike a moving object.

Cues

- Verbal: "Hold," "swing"

Modifications

- Lower the string as needed for ideal height.
- Use a larger object (balloon) for an easier target to be hit.

T-Ball is an introductory game for teaching baseball to students of all levels and ages. It can be modified to increase or decrease difficulty to meet all playing levels. Since most organizations may not have a T-ball set, it is easier to use a large pylon instead. The pylon allows the participant to practice batting without having an object tied to the ceiling or doorway.

Equipment

- Large pylon, foam or rubber ball

Instructions

- A large pylon is used with a foam ball or dodgeball on top.
- Set up the four bases (home, first base, second base, third base) needed for T-ball using markers or smaller pylons. One large pylon is placed in front of home plate. The ball is placed on top of the large pylon.
- Divide the group into two teams or sides. One is batting and the other is fielding. One side can be the teacher in the fielding position (catching) and the student batting or with a bigger group in teams.
- Allow the student multiple tries to hit the ball off the tee. Cueing to then "Drop the bat" and then "Run the bases."
- The student may run all the bases to finish their turn, or they can stay on first base and wait for their teammate to bat.
- Continue this pattern with the next batter until all the students on that team have batted, and then switch teams.
- Rules can be decided by the teacher at the time of the game and the level of the students' playing skills.

Cues

- Verbal: "Swing," "drop the bat," "run the bases"

Modifications

- The larger the ball the easier it is for the participant to hit the ball.

Receiving

As mentioned, receiving skills involve object reception. They involve stopping, securing, or impeding a moving object with the use of the body, body parts, or a piece of equipment. Catching is the most common receiving skill.

Catching

Catching is a more difficult skill to learn than throwing. Catching is receiving and controlling an object. Objects can be of different sizes and weights, arriving at different speeds and from different angles. The best age to begin teaching catching is when the child is four years old. Catching usually develops when children are six to nine years old. With instruction and practice, students can move from an emerging pattern (stage 1) to a developing pattern (stage 2) to a mature catching pattern (stage 3). Figure 4.11 shows emerging (*a*), developing (*b*), and mature (*c*) patterns of catching as catchers improve their execution of the preparation, critical instant, and follow-through phases. Catching has no force production but rather force absorption.

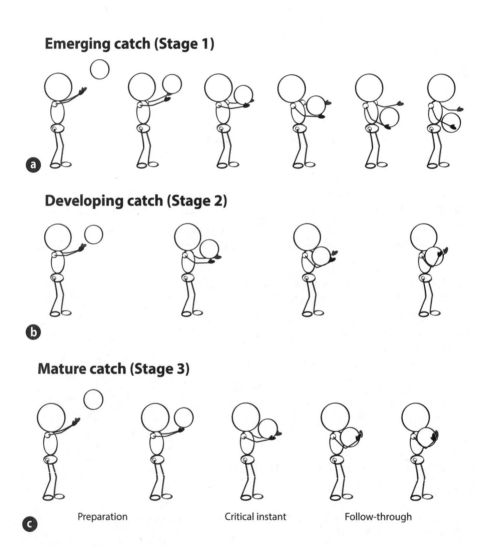

Emerging catch (Stage 1)

Developing catch (Stage 2)

Mature catch (Stage 3)

Preparation   Critical instant   Follow-through

FIGURE 4.11 Growth progression for catching: emerging (*a*), developing (*b*), and mature (*c*) patterns.

Adapted by permission from NCCP, "Fundamental Movement Skills," *Community Leader Workshop–Coach Workbook*, (Coaching Association of Canada: 2018), 44.

Keys to a developing catching pattern:

- Watch the ball until it is in the arms.
- Keep elbows close to body with palms open and up.
- Close arms on ball when it arrives.

Watch for these in the emerging catching pattern:

- Head is turning sideways.
- There is little attempt to close arms around ball.
- Arms are too wide apart to cradle ball.

Adapted by permission from NCCP, "Fundamental Movement Skills," *Community Leader Workshop–Coach Workbook,* (Coaching Association of Canada: 2018), 44.

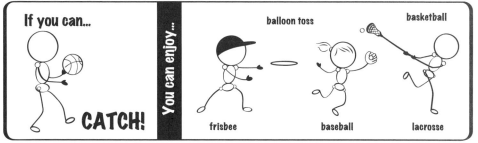

Adapted from Sport for Life, *Developing Physical Literacy: A Guide for Parents of Children Ages 0-12,* (Vancouver: Canadian Sport Centres, 2016). https://sportforlife.ca/wp-content/uploads/2016/12/DPL_ENG_Feb29.indd_.pdf.

Catching Skill Practice

Equipment

- Ball (use various sizes and materials to ensure success)
- Omni balls (because they allow for better grasp)

Instructions

- Have the individual sit on the ground to start.
- Roll the ball to the individual slowly.
- Instruct the individual to use two hands to catch.
- Once the skill is mastered, the individual can then stand up and attempt to catch the ball from standing.
- Cue the individual to keep their hands up (in front of chest).
- Use a bounce pass to throw the ball, then progress to a chest pass movement.

Cues

- Verbal: "Two hands," "hands up"

Modifications

- Modify distance between instructor and individual for greater success.

Polyspot/Pylon Catch

This game challenges the students' ability to catch and throw while also moving to the correct position (polyspot). The students work on coordination, agility, and color recognition. The instructor can increase or decrease the speed that the spots are called in order to meet students' ability.

Equipment

- Three polyspots or pylons

Instructions

- Set up two to three polyspots or pylons of various colors in a row.
- The participant stands on a polyspot or by a pylon, and the instructor will throw the ball to them.
- The participant throws the ball back, and then the instructor calls out or visually cues a different polyspot or pylon and asks the participant to move to the spot. The instructor then throws the ball back and the cycle continues.
- If the participant can tell colors, the instructor can simply call out colors for the individual to move to the corresponding polyspot or pylon.

Cues

- Verbal: "Two hands," "hands up"

Modifications

- To increase difficulty, add more polyspots or pylons or spread out the items in a nonlinear pattern (W pattern).

Trapping/Blocking

Trapping and blocking involve absorbing and controlling the force of an incoming object. The force should be spread over a large surface area for as long as possible.

Keys to trapping:

- Move body directly in the path of the ball.
- Stand with feet apart to create a wide base of support.
- Present a large surface to the incoming ball.
- Watch the ball until contact is made.
- Relax (give) the surface on contact.

Watch for:

- Difficulty lining up body with the ball
- Body is stiff when ball contacts, no give

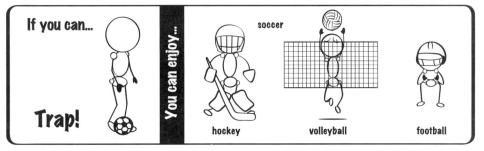

Adapted from Sport for Life, *Developing Physical Literacy: A Guide for Parents of Children Ages 0-12*, (Vancouver: Canadian Sport Centres, 2016). https://sportforlife.ca/wp-content/uploads/2016/12/DPL_ENG_Feb29.indd_.pdf.

Designing Games for Sending Skills and Receiving Skills

Passing a ball (choose a softer ball in order to slow it down) between one person or a group of people is an easy way to introduce the skills in an environment where it is easy to manipulate the skill. For example, you can choose the force used to pass the ball in order to make it easier or harder. Aiming the ball toward the center of the student allows for an easier catch, but if you pass to the less dominant side of the student it allows for crossing of the midline and reaction skills.

Single Equipment Teaching Method

Using a single piece of equipment in games can be a helpful and creative way to help children on the spectrum develop movement skills. A single piece of equipment reduces transition time during the lesson, which allows for more engagement. This method is also a good lead-up to inclusion in a physical education class where there are multiple distractions.

The first decision is to choose a single piece of equipment that most of the students can play with and enjoy playing. Hula-Hoops and playground balls are versatile pieces that most schools or organizations have and can be used to teach many skills. The following lesson plans are based only on using one piece of equipment and can be used one on one or with a small group of children.

Beanbag

GAME	EXPLANATION	FMS
Beanbag tag	• One person is designated as the tagger and tries to tag other students in the room with the beanbag. • Once tagged the beanbag is given to the other player.	• Run • Dodge
Touch this?	• Every student has a beanbag. The instructor calls out the name of an object in the room, and the students run and touch that object with their beanbag.	• Run
Beanbag balance	• The instructor calls out a body part and the students balance or place the beanbag on that body part.	• Stretch • Bend • Rotate
Underhand/ overhand throwing practice	• Practice stepping in opposition and high five buildup to overhand and underhand throwing sequence.	• Throwing • Catching
Obstacle course walk	• Have students place their beanbags in a chosen pattern and try to step only on the beanbags to cross the floor.	• Walk • Dynamic balance • Leap

Hula-Hoop

GAME	EXPLANATION	FMS
Find a hoop	• Lay hoops all around the room. The instructor says to move around the room either independently or with a given skill (skipping, running). The instructor says, "Find a hoop," and then the students need to stand in a hoop. • To increase difficulty, take away one hoop after each round so that more than one student may have to share a hoop.	• Locomotor skills • Balance • Agility • Run • Walk
What can you do with a hoop?	• Ask the students to show the instructor what they can do with a hoop. • Show a few examples, such as jumping in and out, rolling, spinning on the floor.	• Rolling • Bending • Catching • Walk • Run • Agility
Rolling hoops/ Throwing hoops	• Each student has a Hula-Hoop and the instructor then shows them a flat hand in order to roll the hoop upright. • See how far the hoop can roll. • Emphasize a big roll. • Encourage the student to run after the hoop and catch it. • If the space allows one can also throw the hoop up in the air, and the student can try and catch it before it hits the ground.	• Bending • Catching • Rolling • Hand dribble • Walk • Run
Car drive	• Each student has a hoop. • Either the student can stand inside the hoop like being in a car or can use the hoop as a steering wheel. • Have the students move around the room. One can practice going fast or slow, low and high. • Stoplights can also be used by calling out "red" for stop and "green" for go, etc.	• Run • Walk • Twist • Rotate
Close and far	• Each student stands in a hoop, and you practice as a group moving in really close together but only having their hoops touch and then spreading out really far to come back close together. • Instructor can call out "faster" to increase difficulty.	• Walking • Balance • Twist • Rotate • Dodging
Hula-Hoop stretch	• Each student has a hoop and stands in the middle of it. • Have the student reach down and grab the hoop and reach it up over their head.	• Flexibility • Range of Motion

Scarves

GAME	EXPLANATION	FMS
Snowflake freeze tag	• Have one or two students act as taggers. • They each have a scarf, and they tag other students with the scarf. • These tagged students then freeze like a snowflake (arms stretched and legs stretched). • The nontagger students can "unfreeze" these students by tapping on shoulders. Rotate taggers.	• Coordination
Scarf body parts	• Instructor calls out body parts and the students wave the scarf over the body parts.	• Coordination • Bending • Stretching • Rotation
Juggling	• Students can be either sitting, kneeling, or standing. • Show how the hands can take turns "switching" the scarf back and forth between them. • Start small with full grip, and then spread hands farther apart, cueing to get more air or height with the scarf. • Add in more scarves when comfortable or keep at a simple level until mastered.	• Catching
Wall wash	• Using dominant and nondominant hands take turns "cleaning" the walls of the room. • Working cross body as well as cueing "high" and "low," this game works on direction and alternating hands in a simple skill.	• Coordination • Pushing • Stretching • Rotation
Skating	• In a room with a noncarpeted floor place a scarf under each foot and demonstrate how to "skate" carefully on the scarves. • Be careful not to slip. Go slow and steady. • Once comfortable the students can "skate" forward and backward around the room.	• Gliding

Rubber Ball (Bounces)

GAME	EXPLANATION	FMS
Bounce and stop	• Students move around the room bouncing their own ball. • The instructor calls out "Stop," and the students must freeze and hold their ball in their arms. • Students can go fast or slow.	• Dribble • Walk • Twist
Number bounces	• The instructor calls out a number, and the students bounce their ball that number of times.	• Dribble • Catching
How high can you bounce	• Students spread out and try to bounce their ball as high as they can. • Students can also bounce off the wall of the room if the ceiling is low.	• Bounce • Catch • Throw
Partner pass (moving)	• Students pair up and walk back and forth together passing the ball between themselves trying not to drop it. • Or you can have the partners play wall ball and pass the ball back and forth throwing one ball against the wall (Playworks, 2022).	• Walk • Catch • Under-hand throw
Dodgeball reversed	• Place a larger ball (exercise ball) or just an extra ball in the middle of the room and have the students try to throw their ball and hit the larger ball in order to move that larger ball in a certain direction. • Students can be in teams, or everyone can stand in a circle as more of a group effort.	• Throwing • Catching

Gator Ball (No Bounce)

GAME	EXPLANATION	FMS
Roll and tag	• Students roll their balls at other students' feet. • Everyone has a ball while trying to avoid getting hit by the ball.	• Rolling • Running
Body part squish / Push-up	• Instructor calls out a body part, and the students place the ball on that body part and squish down gently. • The instructor can then show how to place the ball under one's chest and then squish the ball down and watch the ball rise up again mimicking a push-up. • Pressure is a great way to relax students with ASD.	• Bend • Twist
Line walk and pass ball	• Have all of the students line up at one end of the room and walk all together in a line, passing one ball back and forth in a line one after the other. • Try cueing at first, but then take it away to see if the students can move the ball as well as move all together at the same pace.	• Walk • Throw • Catch
Human bowling	• Divide the class in half or have one student and one EA do the different tasks. • One student is the "bowling pin" and stands in place, and another student rolls their ball toward their feet. If the student is "hit" they pretend to fall down like a bowling pin onto the floor. • You can then switch the roles of the students.	• Rolling • Walking
Ball roll and stretch	• Students sit on the floor (or in a chair) and roll the ball up and down their legs and arms putting gentle pressure on their body.	• Bend • Rolling • Twist

Racquet and Balloons

GAME	EXPLANATION	FMS
Balloon move and balance	• Have the students move around the gym throwing a balloon up in the air and trying to keep it floating up in the air and not touch the ground.	• Walk • Run • Volleying
Racquet balance	• Have the students hold a racquet in one hand and then place their balloon on top of the racquet and move around the space and not let the balloon fall off the racquet.	• Balance • Walking
Racquet balloon hits	• Have the students practice hitting the balloon with the racquet and try to keep it up in the air.	• Striking
Balloon group passing game	• Play a group game either in a courtlike setting or in a circle and pass one balloon back and forth. • Break into smaller groups for more or less competitive groups.	• Striking • Catching

Using a single piece of equipment reduces transition time for students and develops fundamental movement skills and understanding that transfer to the physical education lesson content. Another way for students on the spectrum to understand physical education activities is to make sense of what each piece of equipment can do and how it relates to the specific game.

Ball Sense

Ball sense is the concept of introducing students to the reasons why a specific ball is used for a specific sport or activity. Ball sense, introduced at the preschool to kindergarten age range, teaches the difference in size, color, and shape and ultimately why that ball is used in that sport.

First, place a soccer ball, basketball, volleyball, baseball, and football all in a row and have the students look at the differences and similarities between all five balls. Asking questions about the size and feel of the balls can lead into what makes each ball good for specific things and poor for others.

Next, have the students take each ball and see what it does best. Which ball is better for hands or feet? Which ball goes up the highest? Kicks the farthest? Bounces the best? This will naturally allow the students to come to their own conclusions as to why each ball works best for a specific sport.

Here are some game examples to try with each ball:

- Kicking
- Bouncing, hitting
- Throwing (one hand)
- Throwing (two hands)
- Catching
- Control of the ball with hands
- Control of the ball with feet

Ball sense gives the child a better overall understanding that will assist in developing sports skills and game understanding.

Go-To Games

This section includes games that can be used for warm-up with an inclusive class, a small group activity with one or more students on the autism spectrum, or one or two students on the spectrum. Importantly, these games incorporate game play with the ABCs and fundamental movement skills. In these games, children get to practice playing games and to develop familiarity with moving in space in relation to others. They also begin to develop tactical understanding of how different kinds of games work (e.g., invading a space). These games and activities are fun for children and adaptable for any age, whether it is an individual or group session, and all ability levels.

Builders and Bulldozers

This game allows participants to practice the skills of pushing and pulling (hand manipulation), spatial awareness, and game play.

Equipment

- Pylons

Instructions

- Pylons are set up in the playing area in a random pattern.
- The instructor asks the participant to push (bulldoze) the pylons over as fast as they can.
- Once all the pylons are knocked over, the instructor will then ask the participant to put up (build) all of the pylons as fast as they can.
- It can be played one on one or with a group.
- Any size of area can be used for this game, depending on the number of participants.
- Emphasize that the participant uses two hands to push or pull the pylons.

- Participants may be tempted to use their feet to kick the pylons over instead of using their hands, because some participants do not like bending over repeatedly.
- Counting (down or up) the number of remaining pylons can help motivate and set expectations so that the participant completes the activity effectively.

Cues

- Use the verbal cues "push" to knock the pylon over and "pull or put up" to put the pylon back up.

Modifications

- The instructor can make the game more difficult by playing the opposite skill (pushing when the participant is pulling or vice versa) in order to create a gamelike atmosphere.
- If the participant understands the function of a bulldozer and a builder, the instructor can ask the participant or group to explain the differences between the two. The instructor can explain that a bulldozer knocks objects (buildings) down and that a builder builds objects (buildings). When explaining about pushing or pulling, demonstrate them at the same time to emphasize the word with the action and to reinforce what is being asked.
- When playing the game with a larger group, divide half the group as builders (putting up) and half as bulldozers (pushing down) and see who can be the fastest. Switch the actions so that the participants get a turn doing both skills. Use a timer to determine how long each game lasts.
- If it is an individual with more physical limitations, you can put it up higher on a table and then have them push it over from there or pull it up. Also one could use a hockey stick for an individual in a wheelchair to push the pylons over.
- If you have a group session where there are multiple ability levels, have some of the faster participants knock over only certain colored pylons and leave the other color for participants who may need more time.

(Physical Educator, 2017)

Clean Up

This game allows the participants to practice picking up and putting down bean-bags (hand manipulation), spatial awareness, running and walking, and cleaning up.

Equipment

- One Hula-Hoop, beanbags, container (optional)

Instructions

- Using one's hands or a container, move the beanbags from the floor to the hoop (bin).
- Emphasize that the participants can only pick up one beanbag at a time.
- The instructor places a hoop or a container in the middle of the playing area. Beanbags are then thrown randomly around the hoop or the container in the playing area. The instructor then tells the participants that they need to clean up all the beanbags and place them into the hoop or container. Once all the beanbags have been cleaned up the game can be played again to see if the time can be improved.

Cues

- Verbal cues: "pick up and put down (or drop)"

Modifications

- This game can be played in a small or large playing area.
- It can be played one on one or with a group.
- To increase the difficulties of this game add another hoop. The hoops are placed at opposite ends of the playing area, and the beanbags are distrib-uted in the middle.
- Divide the participants into two groups, or have the instructor be on one side and the participant on the other side if the game is being played in a one-on-one situation. Make sure the hoops are different colors because it will iden-tify which side the participants are on. An uneven amount of beanbags are thrown in between the hoops in order for one side to have more beanbags than the other, allowing a winner to be determined. Participants will collect one beanbag at a time and drop it into their hoop before returning to pick up another. The participants with the most beanbags in their hoop are the winners.

Stop and Go Locomotor Skills (Red Light, Green Light)

This game allows the participant to practice various locomotor skills (walk, run, skip, jump, etc.) as well as learning to stop and go on command (Playworks, 2022).

Equipment

- Scooters (optional).

Instructions

- Clear a playing area of any obstacles.
- Instruct the participants to move around the room using the chosen locomotor skills. Instruct the participant to go and perform the skill, and then stop when the skill has been practiced 5 to 10 times continuously.
- Choose a new skill and have the participants continue this pattern.
- Five to eight locomotor skills can be performed, depending on the ability of the participants for the duration of the game.

Cues

- Hand signals for the command "stop" can be helpful to reinforce the cue.
- Game concept can be introduced by using colored beanbags (red for stop, green for go, and yellow for slow) as visual cues to go alongside the verbal cues.

Modifications

- This setup will allow the participants to practice moving around the playing area on scooters.

Chicken Toss

The shape and flexibility of the rubber chicken allows the skill of overhand throwing to be practiced with little to no instruction.

Equipment

- Rubber chicken or any rubber animal

Instructions

- Begin by having the participant or group of participants sitting either across from the instructor or in a circle.
- Picking up the rubber chicken (emphasizing holding the rubber chicken by the head) the participant should be instructed to throw the chicken to the instructor or to the other participants in the circle. The instructor should emphasize the participants using each other's names before throwing to them.
- Participants of this age enjoy the noise the rubber chicken makes when it hits the ground.

Cues

- Instruct the participant to pick up the chicken and then throw (verbal cue).
- Typically the participant will use overhand throwing (which is the skill desired) so use the verbal cue "elbow up" to reinforce the skill of overhand throwing.

Modifications

- During a one-on-one session, instruct the participant to throw a desired number of times emphasizing the verbal cue "elbow up."
- The instructor can modify the number of throws and whether the participant sits or stands when throwing. Underhand throwing can also be practiced. If the participant has mastered the skill of overhand or underhand throwing the instructor can add in the skill of stepping in opposition.

Recess and Playground

The ABCs and fundamental movement skills can also be practiced during recess at school and on playgrounds outside school hours. There are some additional considerations for children on the spectrum during recess and playground times.

Most children love recess; however, not all children want to socialize and expend large amounts of energy at recess. For children on the autism spectrum, recess may provide a break and relief from the anxiety of the classroom structure. At school it might be helpful to add in a social story component about recess. The social story can help the child identify what the time can be used for and how. Recess may be a time for the student to decompress and perhaps even stim. It is an unstructured time for the child to wander and move however they feel comfortable. This may allow the child to have less stimming behaviors in the class because they know that this time is coming up where they are allowed to yell or run or stim in order to decompress. The student may enjoy going on the swing for the whole recess, but it could be explained in the social story that one could share the swing or take turns on it with other students.

The playground is another way to keep children physically active and develop ABCs and fundamental movement skills. This also gives them a chance to interact with peers in a nonstructured environment that is supervised by teachers, parents, or caregivers. Children with ASD may have some disadvantages on the playground. They have uncertainty (and anxiety) with many aspects of what is expected on the playground. Having different social skills and little understanding of the "unwritten" rules of socializing, they are at a loss for what to do or how to respond when they find themselves in social situations. They may not understand simple games that the other children are engaged in, and they may not have a sense of how to play with recreational equipment that is used on the playground. Sadly, some of the children do want to interact with their peers and engage in these activities, but they don't know how. Other children may become frustrated with them and don't understand why the children are behaving in a different way. Children with ASD may not know how to initiate play with their peers. They do not have the words, or if they do, they do not know how to approach another child or how to ask if they want to play with them.

Conflict can occur on the playground in the form of pushing, hitting, grabbing, and screaming. Sometimes pushing isn't meant to show aggression at all. Sometimes the child is actually trying to initiate play with another child, but pushing is the only way they know how. It is very important that children learn how to play at a young age and to engage in many different kinds of play. Organized play needs to be arranged as often and as early as possible. Children need to be taught how to use playground equipment and encouraged to become involved in many different types of play.

Teaching children how to play is very important. Structured games and interaction are necessary for children so they understand what to do during free time. If children are left on their own with no instruction, it is very likely that conflict will continue to occur. This takes a lot of effort, but it will make a huge difference in the child's ability to socialize as they continue to mature.

Conclusion

Early childhood is the optimal time for children to learn fundamental movement skills and meet movement milestones. A child entering grade 1 is expected to have mastered the ABCs of physical literacy and a beginning level of fundamental movement skills, which will form the foundation for physical education, recess activities, and playground programs. Families are critically important in teaching and supporting their child to become competent, confident, and motivated to move.

Gymnastics is a common activity done in elementary schools once or twice a year. Most of the equipment consists of climbing obstacles with rope ladders and monkey bars. Abby was a student in grade 1 and had difficulty pulling herself up onto the rings of the equipment due to a lack of grip strength. She was missing out on the activities with her peers because it took her twice as long to get through each station. The rules of the school district stated that educational assistants were not allowed to help her onto the equipment if she was not able to climb up independently. This rule then excluded her from multiple stations where she was not able to pull herself up. Changing the direction of movement from climbing up and over the rungs to under and across allowed her to use the full length of the equipment with her peers but not risk her own safety and allowed her to be independent at each station. She focused more on hanging off the equipment rather than climbing across. The stations were then practiced with an EA in order from 1 to 10 with the same student partner for two sessions. By the third session, she was able to move independently with her peer support from station to station, as well as move independently on the equipment without having aid or verbal cues from the EA. This adaptation turned exclusion into inclusion in physical education for Abby.

Erin Bennett

Physical Education and Community

Many physical education lessons use games and sports to develop physical literacy and motivate children to be active. Developing physical literacy from games offers many opportunities for peer relationships, inclusion, skill development, and fun. Children apply fundamental movement skills and learn the basic strategies of games. Children on the spectrum often avoid, rather than engage in, games. Such avoidance could be due to the noisy, chaotic, and unpredictable nature of the environment or the lack of leaders willing to teach game skills.

This chapter begins by providing suggestions for instruction in teaching games. The key to inclusion in physical education and games is a successful transition from one-on-one teaching to full class participation. Teaching Games for Understanding (TGfU), a model for participants to learn principles of play that are common to most sports and games, will be introduced next (Griffin & Butler, 2005). Games are divided by organization and tactics. Learning games by teaching according to the common organization and tactics creates ease of understanding for students on the spectrum.

The bulk of this chapter provides lesson plans for teaching the most common games and sports used in physical education today, plus some additional activities common in community programs. The final section highlights a program, Soccability, as an example of a successful inclusive community sports program.

Planning for Physical Education

Physical education can be one of the more difficult classes for participation by students on the spectrum. The size of the gymnasium space, lighting, and noise level from equipment or other students can cause disabling anxiety. This can decrease the interest and motivation for the student to participate fully, or even partially, in the class as well as increase the difficulty for the teacher to plan to accommodate all of these external factors. Though these external factors can cause anxieties, there are resources and aids that can decrease the students' sensitivities to the light and noise, such as sunglasses or noise-canceling headphones. It is also very important to keep practicing in these environments, even for a very short period of time, because the setting can contribute to students' overall well-being of being out in the world.

The goal is for the student to participate as much as possible, for the longest period of time, with their peers in the class. Physical education is important in the students' overall development and can help ease anxieties by increasing physical movement.

Physical education allows an opportunity to move freely and release tension in the body. Success in physical education is individual to each student. Success for one student could be staying in the room (not participating) for 15 minutes, whereas success for another student could be doing three activities in the class with peers. Success is defined by the individual and the teacher or educational assistant both knowing and understanding the long-term goal and how the goal is measured. The approach may have to change multiple times in the school year, but it is important to adapt so that the goal can be achieved.

Given the complex nature of teaching physical education and adapting a game or sport to a variety of students of all ability levels, here are some guidelines:

- *Specific activity/movement goal for each class:* When putting together the lesson plan, first consider what game or activity is selected in the curriculum for the next set time period (weeks or month). Next, determine a specific activity, movement, or skill for the student to play or practice. Have a goal in mind, and plan according to the students' interests and ability levels. For example, badminton may be in the curriculum to teach this month, but starting with hitting a balloon in a circle might give greater success and enjoyment before moving on to traditional badminton equipment and nets. The game play and movement pattern are similar to badminton, but balloons may be a better introduction than to simply hand the child a racquet.

- *Consistent routine (start and finish) and class schedule:* The most important part of any lesson plan is a consistent routine to ensure that the student knows and understands what will happen before, during, and after the class. Keeping a consistent routine with set expectations will allow for the greatest success in any teaching setting. A consistent routine helps the student to reduce anxiety, and it helps the teacher as well. Starting and ending the class in the same location or by using the same activity will aid in lesson planning as well as indicate to the student that the class is starting or ending. Students might use a visual schedule for their daily school day, and a schedule specific to physical education can be created if needed.

- *Consistent, simple language:* Keep language short, simple, and repetitive. Instructions should be short and to the point. Use slower speech if the instructions are longer. Make sure to allow the student time to process your instructions before moving on to another set of instructions. An example of "First this, then that" language is helpful in this situation.

- *Games and equipment that the student loves:* Finding a piece of equipment or a game that the student enjoys using or doing can make physical education a fun and rewarding time for both the student and the teacher. The game or equipment can be used throughout the whole class to increase participation and adapted to teach multiple skills and games. A game or equipment piece can also be used as a reward for completion of another task in the class.

- *Break down and build up skill:* Skills need to be broken down to their simplest form, then they can be built up once each skill level is developed and mastered. As mentioned in chapter 2, task progressions allow the student to develop at their own pace. When introducing a new skill, start at the most basic level of the skill. Once that skill is developed, add more complex skills for the student. For example, when teaching how to dribble a basketball, have the student sit on the floor with their legs crossed and instruct them to drop the ball with two hands to the front or side of their body and then catch the ball when it bounces back up. Keep practicing this way until they become more comfortable, and then ask the student to go to kneeling, and so on. This will allow the difficulty to be increased or decreased as needed, enabling the student to develop the skill in their own time and with the best success each time the skill is practiced. If the student starts at a level that exceeds their skill level, then they will not see success as often and may become discouraged with the activity.

- *Practice, practice, practice:* This can apply to a skill or even just to being in the class. The more that is familiar and constant, the better the outcome will be for the student on the spectrum. When practicing a skill, make sure the number of times or length of time is told to the student so that they understand what is being asked of them. For example, if the student is to do five shots on the basketball net, indicate that before they start, or if the student is to spend five minutes shooting on the net before moving on to another activity, have a timer close by for a countdown. This is particularly helpful if they like an activity and only want to do that specific activity in the gym.

- *Flexibility:* Be able to pivot while still staying on the activity goal. As the teacher or educational assistant, keep the student engaged and motivated while keeping any uncontrollable behaviors from occurring during the class. If an activity or other student is causing anxiety, shift activities quickly or divide the group to prevent a situation from occurring. Being able to jump ahead or stay on an activity longer can help maintain the flow of the class. Have a separate area with the same equipment that is being used in the class in case the student needs a break to allow them to participate in the class but in their own comfort zone. When an activity is going well, be flexible and add to the activity in order to progress the skill development. For example, if pylons are of particular interest to the student, keep using them in order to teach throwing, kicking, and various games (e.g., builders and bulldozers). Or if the class is enjoying red light, green light, add in soccer balls to make it a dribbling exercise in a context that the students enjoy. Being able to take the tone of the students and adapt the activity on the spot to have success takes trial and error as well as getting to know the students and their behaviors.

These guidelines will help teachers and educational assistants to plan for success in physical education class. The goal is that every child is participating in some way appropriate to their abilities and physical literacy goals.

Transitioning Activities from One-on-One to Inclusive Group

The quality of life for children is increased when they are included in activities with their classmates, family, and friends. Typically, children will progress from one-on-one instruction, through small groups to larger groups to full game participation.

In a one-on-one session, the leader helps the student become more familiar with the instruction, the skill, and the flow of the class in a less stressful or distracting environment. Behaviors due to environmental factors tend to be the biggest hurdle in full participation for a student on the spectrum; therefore, if these factors can be lessened by practice and familiarity, there is a greater chance for success and meaningful participation for the student. The student may not be interested in the actual activity being played by the group, but the participation alongside their classmates is a greater success than actual game play.

Working up to full game play is a challenge. Start by adding in one or two students at the end of an individual session, and see how it goes. This could be at the beginning or end of the session for as little as 5 to 10 minutes. Select an activity where the student on the spectrum needs to wait their turn and cannot always dictate the activity. Once this has become a meaningful experience for the student, try a small-group game in a gymnasium setting with only 5 to 10 students. This is an activity that hopefully has been practiced from the very beginning in a one-on-one session so that the student fully understands what is expected from them. They may still need to be cued each time it is their turn, but with practice there is hope that cueing will gradually diminish. Try to find an activity or equipment that the student enjoys because this may make it an easier transition to full participation. Adapt the activity to the student, but also maintain rules for turn taking, sharing, and winning.

The transition from one-on-one to full participation can take time, and the leader may need to go back and forth, depending on the activity, sport, or development of the student. Some games may be great in a group, but when a new sport is introduced one may need to return to individual sessions. This is not going backward, it is adapting to the student's needs at that time.

While full inclusion is the goal of all physical education classes, it may be more realistic and more beneficial for the child on the spectrum to begin to engage with classmates in only the warm-up portion or a specific part of the lesson. After the inclusion, the child may continue to learn and refine skills using the ADAPT method in a one-on-one setting or small group.

Teaching Games for Understanding

Teaching Games for Understanding (TGfU) was developed as a model for physical activity leaders to enable participants to become more skillful game players. When a player has a greater understanding of the fundamentals of the game, a more skillful performance during play is developed. By allowing the participant to play the game, this model promotes active involvement in the learning process and gives meaning to play (Griffin & Butler, 2005). The TGfU model for teaching games helps participants to learn tactics and strategies of game play in tandem with technical skill development (Kirk & MacPhail, 2002). The TGfU method also helps students to think critically, solve problems, negotiate ideas with different people, become leaders, develop self-awareness, learn fundamental movement skills, and adapt and transfer learning to different situations (Volleyball Canada, 2017). The TGfU model develops better and more knowledgeable game players, and students are more motivated to take part in a variety of games.

TGfU centers on the use of modified games to adapt to the different developmental levels of each participant (Kirk & MacPhail, 2002). This approach works well with participants on the autism spectrum because modifications can be made to the rules, playing area, and equipment. Skills and techniques are developed by using simple games and drills, but a more complex skill or technique is introduced only when participants reach a more complex level of game play that forces them to learn the skill. Instead of telling the participants that the lesson today is to play soccer, the leader develops simple games where the focus is on playing, with the introduction and practice of the technical skills needed to play soccer interspersed between the games. As the participant develops skills and knowledge, the games can be changed so that the participant is continually challenged in terms of game appreciation, tactical awareness, decision-making, and execution of skills.

TGfU divides games with similar tactics, rules, and skills into four game forms (Hopper, 1998). The game forms listed in table 5.1 will be foundational in the physical education units in the next section.

Table 5.1 TGfU Game Forms

GAME FORM	CHARACTERISTICS	FMS	PE UNIT
Target	Accuracy and control	Throwing	Bowling
			Curling
Net or wall	Participants move, control, and hit an object within a specified space. Participants try to make it difficult for opponents to send the object back to the wall or return it across the net.	Throwing Catching Striking Jumping	Volleyball Badminton
Striking and fielding	Participants can hit, kick, or throw an object (preferably a ball) and then score a run by moving to designated areas. Batting participants create opportunities to score by hitting balls out of an area of play and score by running between safe areas without the ball being caught on the fly by fielding players, or the ball reaching the safe area before the batting players. (Hopper, 1998). Fielders retrieve the object and get it to a specified place to stop runs from being scored and to get opponents out.	Running Striking Throwing Kicking Catching	Kickball T-ball Softball Baseball
Invasion	Participants control an object, keep it away from opponents, and move it into a scoring position in order to attack a goal. Offensive and defensive participants share the same space and try to prevent the other participants from scoring.	Running Throwing Catching Striking Jumping	Soccer Basketball Hockey

This chapter provides teaching support for each of the game forms mentioned in table 5.1. Each unit will contain lesson plans for each of the basic skills using the TGfU game-skill-development method and include keys for teaching those skills. Bonus games are provided for each of the game forms. Refer back to chapter 4 for each of the fundamental movement skills involved in each game form.

Planning the Lesson

Planning is the key to connecting the physical activity or game goal with the lesson to be presented. Planning encourages readiness for multiple situations that may occur and effectively manages the time spent in the gymnasium or playing field.

Here are a few things to consider when planning a TGfU lesson:

- Plan for easier and harder adaptations since the students will progress at different rates. Use the ADAPT method (see chapter 2) to identify the possibilities.

- Use various types of equipment (see chapter 2, Equipment Variability). Use equipment that is appropriate to the age and ability of the students. Children will experience more success and increase their willingness to play.

- Maximize space and equipment. Optimize the number of play areas one can set up to ensure that children can receive a maximum number of contacts. A rope between two basketball nets, a net-free soccer goal, a swing set, or even a string on the floor works as a net. The key is to keep the majority of children active at one time by maximizing the use of space and equipment available.

TGfU Lesson Template

The following is a TGfU lesson template for physical education units. ADAPT is included to tailor the lesson to the students.

TGfU:

Sport:

FMS:

Skills:

Equipment:
- List all equipment for the lesson.

Warm-up: Select simple games to begin moving. Connect the warm-up to the goal skill or game.

Skill 1: Specific focus on a skill that will improve the game. Know and articulate the technical elements of performing the skill.

Individual or small game: Let students experience the game. Include the new skill.

Skill 2: Specific focus on a skill that will improve the game. Know and articulate the technical elements of performing the skill.

Inclusive game: Add in the skill focus to the game.

ADAPT:

   Ability: Adjust skill to ability, develop task progressions.

   Difficulty: Determine if too easy or too difficult, consider changes to equipment.

   Area: Physical space, increase or decrease.

   People: How many for learning? Match abilities or mix.

   Teaching: How to organize and instruct? Cueing. Rule changes. More time.

Cool-down: Reduce activity level. End in the same way.

Evaluation: Safe? Engaged? Success? Skill development?

Diagram: Use this space to draw the area, setup, and movement of the activities.

Adapted by permission from Volleyball Canada, *Elementary Volleyball Teacher Guide,* (Coaching Association of Canada and Volleyball Canada: 2017).

Here are some keys to using the lesson templates:

- Some lessons will take years to develop the skills and complete a whole lesson based on the starting point and motivation of the child. The leader may only use one piece of the lesson.
- Some activities can be done in a group with each child working by themselves to accomplish a task.
- To make the most efficient use of time, select only one to three pieces of equipment for each lesson.
- Use activities that flow together to reduce management time.
- Using the same structure of activities repetitively reduces anxiety for the child.
- Several cool-down ideas are given in the lessons. It is common to run out of time in the classes. The most important part is that the end of the lesson is a consistent routine. Use a verbal cue, such as "reach up toward the sky and now back down to your toes" (leader reaches both hands up to the ceiling and then back down to the toes). Then put your hands together giving the cue, "give yourself a big clap and we are *all done!*"
- There are bonus activities that can be interchanged or used alone for the different lessons.

The suggestions given above are keys to success when implementing physical education lessons. The next section provides lessons for common physical education units grouped by TGfU game forms. Refer to chapter 4 for the keys to teaching the fundamental movement skills (FMS) specific to each lesson.

TGfU Lessons

As indicated in chapter 4, many activities are based on the ABCs and fundamental movement skills. If a child can run, throw, catch, balance, jump, and strike, the opportunities for engaging in game activities in physical education, family life, and community are endless.

Target Games

Target games are games where the goal is accuracy and control of an object to a specified target. Lesson plans for bowling and curling are provided.

Bowling

Adaptations for bowling include remaining in a stationary position, reducing the number of steps, using two hands instead of one, using a ramp, and using a partner. The leader can give continuous verbal cues throughout the movement (Stopka, 2006).

Skills needed: comfortable grip, footwork rhythm, and release timing
FMS: Balance, coordination, throwing

Bowling Lesson 1

TGfU: Target

Sport: Bowling

FMS: Throwing

Skills: Comfortable grip, release timing

Equipment:

- Tennis ball
- Exercise ball or larger playground ball
- Small foam balls

Warm-up: *Tennis ball tag.* Give one student a tennis ball and have them tag the other students. Once tagged with the ball that student now becomes the tagger and continues on with the game. You can encourage that the students tag using a low-five hand motion so that it mimics rolling the ball.

Skill 1: *Tennis ball catch and squeeze.* Give students a tennis ball and have them bounce and catch it themselves. Students can sit on the ground or kneel or stand and do this activity.

Individual or small game: *Tennis ball roll and catch.* Have the students continue with the tennis ball, but have the students face a wall and start to roll the ball back and forth catching and releasing the ball. Try the same activity with a slightly bigger ball. The students can also break into pairs and roll the ball back and forth with good grip form.

Skill 2: Each student is given a foam ball. Have the students squish the ball with various body parts. Then have the students move on to squeezing it with their hands and fingers. This will really work on their grip strength.

Inclusive game: *Move the middle.* Place a large exercise or playground ball into the middle of the room. Split the group into two groups on either side of the room. The goal is to move the exercise ball past a line or marker on either team's side. Students use a small tennis ball or foam ball and throw it at and move the bigger ball. Once it passes the marker or line it counts as one point for the other team.

ADAPT:

A: Catching and throwing with one hand (bouncing the ball). Two hands can be used to start, or use one hand, but keep the distance between the ball and ground small. Reinforce the low-five arm motion for throwing the ball.

D: Vary the size and texture of the ball. Bring the student closer or move them farther away. They can do activities sitting, kneeling, or standing.

A: The area needs to have enough wall space for the number of students as well as enough moving area for the exercise ball.

P: This can be one-on-one activity or a group activity.

T: Use the cue "squish" or "squeeze" the ball or fingers. Low five is used to cue the arm motion for the roll.

Cool-down: Form a circle with the students, and pass a small foam ball around the circle to cool down.

Evaluation: Safe? Engaged? Success? Skill development? Were the students able to control the ball in the correct manner? Were they able to squish or squeeze the ball with their hands or fingers? Were they able to catch the ball quickly when the ball was in motion?

Bowling Lesson 2

TGfU: Target

Sport: Bowling

Skill: Footwork rhythm

Equipment:
- Polyspots
- Pylons
- Beanbags

Warm-up: Practice knocking over small pylons in order to get the slide motion of the back foot in. Set up 10 to 12 pylons in a small area, and have the students move around the area knocking them over with the palm of their hand.

Skill 1: Use polyspots to mark the number of steps needed to take before one releases the ball. For right-handed bowlers, start with the polyspot in front of the left foot, then move to the right foot and then the left. For left-handed bowlers, start with the poly spot in front of the right foot, then move to the left foot and then the right. A fourth polyspot (polyspot of a different color to indicate a change in movement for the slide) is put to the side of the dominant foot to encourage the participant to slide the polyspot back using one's foot. Have the students take individual turns on the same polyspots, or use a set for each student.

Individual or small game: Place a marker (pylon) in the middle of a hoop at the farthest end of the playing space. Place different markers (Hula-Hoops or smaller pylons) at varying distances from the main marker and hoop. Participants then try to throw an object (like beanbags or small balls) toward the main marker and hoop from the designated smaller markers around the playing space. A point is given if the participant gets the object in the hoop and two points if the marker is hit.

Skill 2: Make a circle with the group and have a polyspot in front of each student. Cue the student to "step" onto the polyspot and then "roll" the ball to another student in the circle. Ensure that each student gets a chance to roll the ball.

Inclusive game: Pins. Form a circle using bowling pins or pylons. It should be approximately two feet in diameter. Three lines are formed from the circle with distances at 9 feet, 15 feet, and 20 feet. Participants throw a beanbag into the circle without knocking any pins down from all three distances.

ADAPT:

A: Add an implement for a child who may need assistance reaching pylons. Change the size and weight of the ball to increase success.

D: Move the targets closer or farther away to increase or decrease difficulty.

A: The playing area can be moved to up against a wall to decrease the area the balls can roll away.

P: Use one-on-one or group instruction.

T: Use smaller groups or individual activities in order to increase opportunities to participate.

Cool-down: Place a pylon close to the cleanup area or equipment room, and have the students roll a foam ball with proper form and try to hit the target before the ball is put away.

Evaluation: Safe? Engaged? Success? Skill development? Did the student step in opposition when throwing the ball? Was it a fluid or hand-over-hand motion?

BONUS

Frisbee Toss

Equipment:
- Two pylons
- Two Frisbees

Description: Set two pylons 10 to 15 feet apart. Two teams are created, and one team member from each team stands near each pylon. Each pylon will have team members with two Frisbees. Participants will take turns throwing their Frisbees and attempt to land their Frisbee closest to the pylon.

Adaptations:
- *Simple:* Allow participants to stand closer to the pylons. Use beanbags, paper plates, or pail lids instead of Frisbees.
- *Difficult:* Vary the manipulations used, such as kicking instead of throwing, Hula-Hoops instead of pylons, and using an implement like a hockey stick.

Wall Bowling

Equipment:

- Gym floor tape

Description: Instruct participants to roll their ball toward a variety of tape marks on the wall. Tape can also be placed on the floor, and the participants must roll their ball over the marks.

Pick a Pin

Equipment:

- Bowling pins
- Balls

Description: Participants are divided into pairs and given four bowling pins per pairing. The pins are set up in an even fashion for the participants' ability and are set up a fair distance away for the participants to roll the ball. Some participants are able to handle greater distances, but others may require a closer distance. One partner will roll first (bowler), and the other partner will choose which bowling pin to knock down (caller). It may be helpful if the pins are all different colors. Once the bowler has knocked down all the pins, the roles are reversed, and the bowler becomes the caller and the caller becomes the bowler.

Adaptations:

- *Simple:* Use a smaller number of bowling pins. Use a larger ball to roll toward the pins. Reduce the distance.
- *Difficult:* Have participants try to knock down two pins at a time instead of just one.

Lawn Bowling (Outside) or Bocce

Equipment:

- Play balls of different colors

Description: Use playground balls; one is a different color

Curling (Off Ice)

Skills needed: Throwing the rock, sweeping the rock, and aiming at a target
FMS: Balance and coordination

Curling Lesson

TGfU: Target

Sport: Curling

FMS: Balance and coordination

Skill: Throwing the rock and sweeping

Equipment:

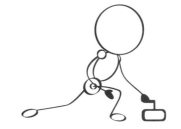

- Frisbees
- Pylons
- Scooters
- Soccer ball
- Beanbag

Warm-up: Each student will have a scooter and will line up against a wall. Allow the students to kneel or lie down on the scooter. Tell the students to see how far they can slide their scooter. Students need to stay on the scooter the whole time and keep their hands out of the way.

Skill 1: Kneeling on a small scooter, keep one foot on the ground push off the wall several times to practice keeping a straight line while pushing off. Drag the foot behind the scooter. This takes good core strength and flexibility. Practice twisting the rock while releasing the rock (if available, or use a Frisbee).

Individual or small game: Students practice sliding Frisbees across the floor toward a target (pylon or ball). See who can make it the closest.

Skill 2: Sweeping requires quick eye-hand movements and balance. Since the students are not on the ice it is a different skill. Sweeping the rock in a gymnasium is a good team practice and a good opportunity to practice verbal cues between students.

Adapted from "How to Play," FloorCurl, accessed December 1, 2022, www.floorcurl.com/how-to-play.

Inclusive game: Divide the students into sweepers and throwers. Have half of the students throw the "rock," and then have the sweepers place a marker (beanbag) where the "rock" lands. See which student can get the rock the farthest. Use a Frisbee if a curling rock on wheels isn't available.

ADAPT:

A: Students may or may not be able to balance on the scooter or may get distracted by being on the scooter. Redirection may be needed.

D: If the scooter is too distracting consider using a polyspot instead, and have the student move the Frisbee on its own.

A: Use a space where the Frisbees will be able to slide easily across the floor.

P: This can be an opportunity for full inclusion because students can work together to push a student on the scooter, and then that student throws the "rock." This can also be done in a one-on-one setting.

T: Demonstrating the activity may provide excitement and incentive for using a scooter. Use hand-over-hand instruction for throwing if needed.

Cool-down: Students each have their own scooter board. A soccer ball is used. Students try to hit the soccer ball with the scooters.

Evaluation: Safe? Engaged? Success? Skill development? Is the student able to balance on the scooter with ease?

Net and Wall Games

Participants move, control, and hit an object within a specified space. Participants try to make it difficult for opponents to send the object back to the wall or return it across the net. Lesson plans for badminton and volleyball are provided, with bonus games for each.

Badminton

Skills needed: Grip, stance, swing, and footwork
FMS: Coordination and striking

Badminton Lesson 1

TGfU: Net or wall

Sport: Badminton

FMS: Coordination

Skills: Grip and swing

Equipment:
- Racquets
- Balloons
- String
- Broom

Warm-up: Each student is given a racquet. Place the racquet in the dominant hand and have the students walk around "shaking hands" with the racquets with other students. This will reinforce the proper holding grip for the students.

Skill 1: Give each student a balloon and have them try to keep the balloon up in the air for as long as possible.

Individual or small game: Participants are divided into pairs or groups of three and are given one balloon per group. The goal for the pair or group is to keep the balloon up in the air for as long as they can, keeping it up off the ground. Each hit of the balloon is counted, and participants keep counting until the balloon is dropped. Pairs or groups can try to beat their score (how many times they would touch the balloon and keep it off the ground).

Skill 2: Tie the balloon or shuttlecock to a hockey stick or broom. This will allow the students to hit the object more effectively in order to get more practice in. This can be done individually or in pairs.

Inclusive game: Practice throwing a balloon or ball back and forth over a net with two students per side. This lets the students practice moving on a court and getting into position to catch and retrieve the ball.

ADAPT:

A: Use a racquet or object that is appropriate for the student to hold onto. Use nothing if that is easier for the child to use their hand to hit the balloon. Participants are allowed to catch balloons in between throws if too difficult. If this is too easy, use one hand to keep the balloon up.

D: Should the racquet be too heavy, cut a pool noodle into thirds and give the student a piece to hit the balloon. A Ping-Pong racquet will also be easier to connect with the balloon as the distance is shorter from hand to contact point.

A: Needs a space with higher ceilings and not outside due to wind.

P: Can be a fully adapted lesson because you ensure that each side has the same number of skill sets. Using different equipment can help include everyone.

T: Decrease the space and make more groups so students have more opportunity to hit.

Cool-down: Pass the balloon or ball in a circle working on having quick hands and reactions.

Evaluation: Safe? Engaged? Success? Skill development? How easy is it to hit the balloon? Would a shuttlecock be more appropriate?

Badminton Lesson 2

TGfU: Net or wall

Sport: Badminton

FMS: Coordination

Skill: Stance

Equipment:
- Racquets
- Shuttlecocks
- Balloons
- Skipping rope

Warm-up: *Line tag*. Most gymnasiums will have lines on the floor. Students must stay on a line. Once tagged, the person becomes a tagger. Use the badminton court lines to learn the boundaries.

Adapted from K. Boulton, "Line Tag," Elementary P.E. Games, accessed December 1, 2022, https://elementarypegames.weebly.com/line-tag.html.

Skill 1: Students are to move around the gym with pylons set up randomly. Have students move either fast or slow with their feet.

Individual or small game: Divide group into pairs. Give each group a small playing area that is divided by a line or a skipping rope. Participants face each other with a divided line between them. One participant first bounces the balloon or ball in their own space and then hits it with the palm of their hand into the other participant's square. The ball is allowed to bounce in the other participant's square, and that participant returns the ball with the palm of their hand.

Skill 2: Each participant has a badminton racquet in their dominant hand. If the participants are unsure just ask them which hand they eat with or write with. Participants hold the shuttlecock in their nondominant hand. Instruct the participant to straighten the arm in front of them that is holding the shuttlecock. The racquet hand then taps the shuttlecock three times in a row. Use the verbal cue "tap, tap, tap, let go!" The participant then lets the shuttlecock go, and the racquet arm will hit the shuttlecock launching it into the air.

Inclusive game: Participants play a regular badminton game but use balloons instead of a shuttlecock because balloons move slower and are easier to hit for most participants. Move to a shuttlecock when appropriate.

Adaptations:

- *Simple:* Lower the nets, and have the server move closer. Do not use the service court, but allow the serve to go anywhere in the court.

Adapted from "Balloon Badminton," Fit Kids Healthy Kids, accessed December 1, 2022, https://fkhk.sportmanitoba.ca/node/143.

ADAPT:

A: Evaluate if a racquet will be helpful or not to the lesson. Rubber chickens or the palm of your hand can work just as well.

D: Add in a racquet and a shuttlecock when skills are appropriate. Balloons allow more time to react and are an easier target to hit.

A: Keep the area open so that when the racquets are swinging they do not harm anyone.

P: One-on-one or in pairs is best. Small groups are good as well because a larger group can become boring.

T: For the skipping rope game, the item can be passed further back or close to the line in order to reinforce the idea that standing in the middle of the court is the place to be in the space to have the best chance at short or deep balloons or balls . If the instructor feels it is appropriate, they can ask probing questions to assist understanding from the participants.

Cool-down: Use the racquet or rubber chicken to stretch out at the end of the session. Use two hands to hold onto the item.

Evaluation: Safe? Engaged? Success? Skill development? Is the racquet appropriate? Is the balloon appropriate? Is the game play fair and understood or is it hand-over-hand instruction?

BONUS

Tennis Ball Bounce

Equipment:
- Balls that bounce

Description: Divide a smaller playing area into two equal parts. Participants face each other with a divided line between them. One participant first bounces the ball in their own square then hits it with the palm of their hand into the other participant's square. The ball is allowed to bounce in the other participant's square and then the participant returns the ball with the palm of their hand.

Adaptations:
- *Simple:* Participants can use two hands instead of just one open-palmed hand.

Volleyball

Volleyball is a complex game. The traditional skills are difficult but can be adapted for learning. Adaptations include modifying the ball that is used, the size of the courts (smaller, larger, narrower, wider), lowering the height of the net, changing the initial starting point of the server (closer or farther from the net), changing the initial receiving position (closer or farther from the server or starting point), allowing the ball to bounce, number and role of the players involved in the play (add receivers, hitters, blockers).

Skills needed: Volley and setting, passing, serving, hitting, and blocking
FMS: Balance, coordination, catching, throwing, striking, jumping, movement, and skill sequence

Volleyball Lesson 1

TGfU: Net or wall

Sport: Volleyball

FMS: Striking, throwing, jumping

Skills: Volley and setting

Equipment:
- Volleyballs
- Balloons

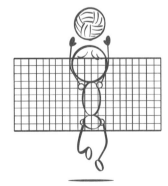

- Balls that rebound
- Rope or net

Warm-up: *Line tag.* Students must stay on a line. Once tagged, the person becomes a tagger. Use the volleyball court lines to learn the boundaries.

Adapted from K. Boulton, "Line Tag," Elementary P.E. Games, accessed December 1, 2022, www.elementarypegames.weebly.com/line-tag.html.

Skill 1: Throw a ball with two hands overhand. Pull arms back behind head for back-swing. Extend arms forward with elbows facing forward. Toss to self then catch overhead. Contact and release the ball with two hands overhead (set). Form an open-circle shape with hands. Thumbs facing opposite ears. Ball is round, not flat.

Begin with balloons or light ball. Use a wall target or basketball hoop to aim for height. Add a partner to increase difficulty.

Individual or small game: Participants are paired up into teams of two. A balloon is given to each pair. The pair can keep the balloon up off the ground as long as they can, contacting the balloon above their heads.

Skill 2: Wally ball. Form partners. Each team of two has one ball. Partners stand side by side facing a wall. Begin by each player taking a turn throwing the ball overhead toward the wall and catching their own ball. Progress to one partner throwing to the wall and other partner catching the ball. Focus on moving their body to get in line with the ball.

Inclusive game: *Two-on-two game.* A team of two plays against another team of two. A line or rope or net can be used to divide the two teams. A balloon or light ball is given to the group of four. Each team tries to do two touches (one for each person) before the balloon or light ball is sent back to the other team.

ADAPT:

A: Can allow catches between contacts in keep-it-up games.

D: Use a lighter ball. Use a bigger ball. Use a ball with a grip for easier catching.

A: Reduce the space if unsuccessful. Increase the distance as competency increases.

P: Begin with activities one-on-one or to oneself. Add a partner.

T: Use physical prompting for teaching extension of the elbows and shape of the hands. Cue to hold the hands up on follow-through.

Cool-down: In a circle have the participants raise their arms up above their heads and stretch. Then reach down to their feet and stretch.

Evaluation: Safe? Engaged? Success? Skill development? Is the contact above the head? Are the hands round not flat?

Volleyball Lesson 2

TGfU: Net or wall

Sport: Volleyball

FMS: Catching, coordination, striking

Skill: Passing

Equipment:
- Volleyball
- Balloons
- Rope or net

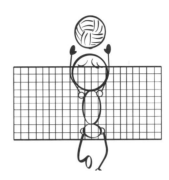

Warm-up: Participants are instructed to move around the room using any movement pattern they choose. This could be running, walking, galloping, or skipping. The instructor then calls out "high" or "low," and the participants need to move either as tall as possible ("high") or as close to the floor as possible ("low"). Other instructions can be added like moving sideways or zig zags.

Skill 1: One-on-one or in a pair. Throw the ball to partner with two hands underhand at waist level. Progress to pass the ball with two arms underhand (forearm pass). Heel of hands together. Thumbs facing down. Arms outstretched. Begin with balloon or light ball. Can also work against the wall.

Individual or small game: One-on-one throwing and catching over a line, rope, or net. See how many times the ball can be thrown back and forth. Try to make the catch below the waist by moving to get in line with the ball. Try to throw the ball overhand.

Skill 2: *Move to the ball.* In pairs facing each other (one back to the net and the other in the court), the student at the net:
- Rolls ball (making partner move from side to side) to the other who catches the ball with the arms fully straight and returns the ball to partner by throwing the ball like a rainbow.
- Rolls ball to partner who catches the ball between the legs and returns it. Alternate with other smaller types of balls (tennis, beanbags). Participants switch positions once a specified number of rolls are complete.

Inclusive game: Groups of three and place a rope, line, or net between the groups. Use a balloon or soft ball. Play starts with a throw over the net, catch or pass with forearms, then volley overhead over the net.

ADAPT:

A: Pair a participant with a peer. If more appropriate cueing and probing is needed, pair with an EA.

D: Balloons slow the object down and allow more time.

A: Reduce the area if limited success getting the ball over the line or net.

P: Transition from one-on-one to pairs to threes as students become successful.

T: Use physical prompting for correct arm and contact position. Use the cue "thumbs down."

Cool-down: Participants can move around the space in high or low space, reaching up and down in space to stretch.

Evaluation: Safe? Engaged? Success? Skill development? Does the student move to get behind the ball and low to contact below the waist, on the forearms with joined hands?

Volleyball Lesson 3

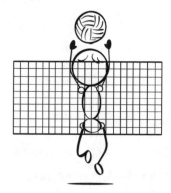

TGfU: Net or wall

Sport: Volleyball

FMS: Coordination, throwing, striking

Skill: Serving

Equipment:
- Beach ball
- Volleyball
- Balloons
- Beanbags

Warm-up: Begin the lesson with everyone standing in a line. Have all of the participants give a high five to the instructor. Repeat two to three times to reinforce the skill. Then have the participants spread out and play high-five tag. Everyone runs around and attempts to give as many high five tags in the allotted time. Repeat playing low-five tag.

Skill 1: Underhand serving. Hit a ball with one hand underhand (serve).

Begin with an arm swing. Demonstrate a low five. Line the participants up in a line, but this time have the participants give a low five to the instructor three to five times. Then add a beanbag into each participant's hand and have them practice the same movement. Add a balloon to the same movement and then finally a ball.

Individual or small game: Participants are paired up into teams of two. A balloon is given to each team. The team must keep the balloon up in the air. Play is started with a low-five contact on the balloon. Participants take turns hitting the balloon up, keeping it off the ground. Participants count the number of times they can keep the balloon up.

Skill 2: Overhand serving. Begin with arm swing. Demonstrate a high five (simple motion).

For added power, pull the hitting arm back in a bow and arrow position, with thumb down and elbow up.

- Hold the ball in front of the hitting shoulder in the open palm.
- Step toward the net with the nondominant foot.
- Feet are facing forward into the court.
- Step, lift ball, and high-five the ball, in one continuous motion.
- Shoulders should finish parallel to the net.

Begin with a balloon, then a soft ball, then a volleyball.

Inclusive game: Divide the group into two. Use a skipping rope or pylons or a net if possible to divide the two teams. Set a target number of passes between the group. They should try to attain the target number in the time allotted. Allow for extra bounces or catches. Start each new sequence with an underhand or overhand serve.

ADAPT:

A: Start with small simple cues. Hold the ball or balloon for the student when serving to increase their chance of hitting.

D: Difficulty can be increased or decreased by changing equipment from a beanbag to a balloon and then finally to a ball.

A: Decrease the height or distance that is needed for the ball to move.

P: Individual attention, or even partner work, may be needed when first starting. A small group will work better once the skill is more fluid and hand-over-hand instruction is not needed.

T: Allow for catching or multiple bounces. Lower the net or remove it completely.

Cool-down: Walking around the volleyball court. Use the commands "Stretch tall" (reach with arms), "Make small" (lower body), "Swing low" (arms like passing), "Swing high" (arms like volleying), and "Goodbye" (wave).

Evaluation: Safe? Engaged? Success? Skill development? Is there a solid underhand or overhand contact? Does the ball go straight?

Volleyball Lesson 4

TGfU: Net or wall

Sport: Volleyball

FMS: Jumping, striking

Skills: Hitting and blocking

Equipment:

- Volleyball
- Balloons
- Polyspots
- Rope

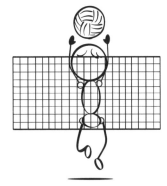

- Basketball hoop
- Net or line

Warm-up: *Lava game.* Lines on the floor are lava. Instruct the participants to move around the space. If there are lines on the floor, instruct the participants to jump or leap over the lines. If the line is touched, a "motivation" of an exercise like jumping jacks is given. You can also swap out like tag, and if you touch the line you are it.

Skill 1: Hitting a ball with one hand overhead (spike). High five at the highest point.
- Jump with two feet horizontally forward.
- Quickly move the body underneath the ball.
- Start with Batman position. Arms backswing. Move the arms up to the Superman position, arms high above head.
- Draw the dominant arm back and the nondominant arm high in front like Robin Hood with his bow and arrow.
- Swing the dominant arm forward, leading with the elbow.
- Connection made with the ball at 12 o'clock. Reach high and bend wrist forward as if reaching into a cookie jar. Use the verbal cues of "Batman", "Superman", "Robin Hood" and "Cookie Monster" to learn the correct sequence of movements.
- Hold the ball and let the student hit. Suspend a balloon or light ball from a doorframe.
- To increase difficulty, add steps to hit the ball.

Individual or small game: Place polyspots in front of each participant. Have the participants stand on their polyspot and attempt to jump as high as they can on the spot. Try a little jump and a big vertical jump, keeping their feet on the polyspot.

Skill 2: To learn blocking, stand facing the wall with a volleyball in both hands above the head. Push the ball with both hands into the wall with open hands and thumbs facing the sky. Add a jump with two feet vertical, and press the ball overhead to the wall. Hold the ball facing the student, and let the student press it back to you. Suspend the balloon or light ball from a doorframe or basketball hoop. Jump vertically to touch the ball with both hands.

Inclusive game: *Three-on-three or four-on-four games.* Participants are divided into groups of three or four depending on the size of the class. Ensure that teams are equal in numbers. Participants play a more traditional game of volleyball but in a smaller group for increased playing time and contacts for each participant. Use extra antennae or pool noodles to divide the net into smaller sections for the small sided games. The ball pattern in the traditional game travels to the net, along the net, and over the net. The skill sequence is serve, pass, set, spike, and block.

ADAPT:

A: Begin with high five. Add the jump. The arm pattern is difficult. Advance when they can high five and jump consistently.

D: Balloons slow action down. Holding a stationary ball allows the student to be concerned only with their action. For the inclusive game, allow the participants to catch the first contact on their team, throw to a teammate closer to the net, who throws it to the third teammate who hits the ball over.

A: Reduce the distance in game play when balls are dropping between players.

P: Progress to up to four-on-four only if success at one-on-one and two-on-two.

T: Cue "Batman," "Superman," "Robin Hood," and "Cookie Monster."

Cool-down: Bounding with two feet for one lap around half the volleyball court. Swing arms from Batman position to Superman position.

Evaluation: Safe? Engaged? Success? Skill development? Can the student jump vertically with arm swing and leg bend to extension? Is the contact with the dominant arm strong? Can the student jump and press the ball with both hands?

BONUS

Bounce Ball

Equipment:

- Balls that bounce

Description: Define a line and space that are appropriate for the ages and ability of the group. Participants face each other on opposite sides of the line. One participant bounces the ball on their own side so that the other participants can catch the ball in the air. The ball cannot touch the ground before the catch. The other participant bounces the ball back immediately from where they caught the ball.

Adaptations:

- *Simple:* Allow for double bounces and so that the ball can touch the ground.
- *Difficult:* Count the number of catches in a row. See if they can challenge themselves.

Roll and Throw

Equipment:
- Volleyball and other types of balls

Description: In pairs facing each other (one back to the net and the other in the court), the child at the net:
- Rolls the ball (making partner move from side to side) to the other, who catches the ball with the arms fully straight and returns the ball to the partner by throwing the ball like a rainbow.
- Rolls the ball to partner, who catches the ball between the legs and returns it. Alternate with other smaller types of balls (tennis, beanbags). Switch positions.

Adaptations:
- *Simple:* Reduce distance between partners.
- *Difficult:* Throw ball to partner, who forearm passes the ball.

Stepping Back

Equipment:
- Volleyballs

Description: With a partner, each player stands approximately 8 feet on each side of the net.
- Player 1 serves the ball over the net to partner, who catches the ball.
- Player 2 serves the ball back over the net to partner.
- When a player successfully serves the ball three times in a row, they take one giant step back to gradually serve from behind the endline.

Adaptations:
- *Simple:* If the server cannot serve three in a row over the net, take one step forward until successful. Have the receiver allow the ball to bounce and then catch the ball.

Striking or Fielding Games

Striking or fielding games involve running, striking, throwing, kicking, and catching. Participants can hit, kick, or throw an object, then score runs by advancing to designated areas. Batting participants create opportunities to score by hitting balls out of an area of play, and they score by running between safe areas without the ball being caught on the fly by fielding players, or the ball reaching the safe area before the batting players. Fielders retrieve the object and get it to a specified place to stop runs from being scored and to get opponents out.

Kickball

Skills needed: Kicking, throwing, catching
FMS: Kicking, throwing, catching, running

Kickball Lesson 1

TGfU: Striking or fielding

Sport: Kickball

FMS: Kicking

Skill: Kicking

Equipment:

- Playground balls (various sizes)
- Pylons
- Polyspots

Warm-up: Form a circle with the group and kick a ball back and forth. Emphasize stepping in opposition. Lines in the gym floor or polyspots can be placed in front of the participants.

Skill 1: Place three sets of pylons in three varying distances. Divide the group into pairs, and have the pairs take turns passing the ball back and forth. Emphasize "big" kicks and "little" kicks.

Individual or small game: Participants line up in front of a pylon. A leader or participant can act as the pitcher and return the ball once it has been kicked. Participants take turns kicking the ball. Start with a stationary ball and then start by rolling the ball to the student from a close distance, and then back up farther as skill improves.

Skill 2: Participants line up in a row at one end of the playing area and practice kicking the ball as far as they can.

Inclusive game: Play a more simplified game of kickball where there are only participants batting (kicking). The leader acts as the pitcher and rolls the ball to the participants. Do not have the students run the bases. This is to practice kicking.

ADAPT:

   A: Consider the skill set of the student by allowing more time to execute the kick.

   D: Increase the size of the ball to make it easier, or decrease the size to make it harder.

   A: Decrease the space between the pitcher and the kicker.

   P: Students can work one on one in pairs or as a group in the game.

   T: Emphasize stepping in opposition when kicking. Use a sticker on the shoe if needed.

Cool-down: Place the ball bin in the center of the room, and have the participants kick their ball toward the target and clean up at the same time.

Evaluation: Safe? Engaged? Success? Skill development? Is the kicking motion fluid? Is stepping in opposition automatic?

Kickball Lesson 2

TGfU: Striking or fielding

Sport: Kickball

FMS: Catching, throwing

Skills: Catching and throwing

Equipment:
- Playground ball
- Different-colored pylons or polyspots

Warm-up: Standing in a circle, pass a ball around, calling out different participants' names. You can increase the speed and distance by increasing the circle size.

Skill 1: Pair participants up and have them practice catching and throwing. Start close and then spread out.

Individual or small game: Set up pylons or polyspots in a baseball field setup. It is preferable to use different-colored markers so that the participants can differentiate between the bases (home, first, second, third). Have the participants move around as a group to show which pylons or polyspots are which bases. Once participants are familiar with the bases the instructor calls out various bases, and the participants move to the called base.

Skill 2: Have the participants stand on a base and practice throwing and catching between bases. Multiple baseball fields may need to be set up to accommodate the group.

Inclusive game: Split the group into two teams. One team is in the outfield and the other team is up to bat. The instructor can be the pitcher for both teams or each team can designate their pitcher. Have pylons or polyspots set up as home plate, first base, second base, and third base. The instructor may want to review the direction of where the students move throughout the bases prior to the game. Have the students each take a base and one in the middle as the pitcher. The other students line up behind home plate. The pitcher rolls the ball slowly or quickly depending on the batter. The batter kicks the ball, and then the other outfielders try to pick up the kicked ball as quickly as possible while the batter moves around the bases as quickly as possible. The instructor can allow for more time needed, depending on the ability level of the students to move. This is continued until all the batters have had a chance to kick the ball, and then the sides switch and continue in their new role.

ADAPT:

A: Start sitting on the ground if catching is more difficult. Then progress to standing.

D: Use a larger soft ball that is easier to catch. Use a larger softer ball that is easier to kick.

A: Decrease the size of the kickball field in order to increase catching success.

P: This game can be played with a variety of ability levels if participants with various ability levels play different positions.

T: Emphasize using two hands to catch. Take out home base and just use first, second, and third. Participants can walk instead of running to the bases. Call the bases out for the batter.

Cool-down: Participants can walk slowly around the bases two to three times doing slow arm circles to stretch out the upper body.

Evaluation: Safe? Engaged? Success? Skill development? Is the kicking accurate? Are the students able to catch the ball?

Kickball Lesson 3

TGfU: Strike or field

Sport: Kickball

FMS: Running

Skill: Running

Equipment:
- Playground ball
- Different-colored pylons or polyspots

Warm-up: Set up the markers in a baseball diamond shape, then have the participants warm up by running around the shape of the field.

Skill 1: This section is repeated because game play is an area that can cause a lot of difficulty for participants on the spectrum. Set up pylons or polyspots in a baseball field setup. It is preferable to use different-colored markers so that the participants can differentiate between the bases (home, first, second, third). Have the participants move around as a group to show which pylons or polyspots are which bases. Once participants are familiar with the bases, the instructor calls out various bases, and the participants move to the specified base.

Individual or small game: Have the participants practice running as fast as they can around the "bases" (pylons or polyspots.) Place the pylons the same distance apart that the bases would be spaced on the field.

Skill 2: Place polyspots or markers on the floor or field. Place one for each participant, and have them practice changing directions quickly. The participants move toward the marker and then place one foot on that marker and quickly pivot to the other direction.

Inclusive game: Split the group into two teams. One is in the outfield and the other is up to bat. This can be done with the instructor being the pitcher and the participants being either the outfielders or the batters. Have pylons or polyspots set up as home plate, first base, second base, and third base. The instructor may want to review the direction of where the students move throughout the bases prior to the game. Have the students each take a base and one in the middle as the pitcher. The other students line up behind home plate. The pitcher rolls the ball slowly or quickly depending on the batter. The batter kicks the ball and then the other outfielders try to pick up the kicked ball as quickly as possible while the batter moves around the bases as quickly as possible. The instructor can allow for more time needed depending on the ability level of the students to move. This is continued until all the batters have had a chance to kick the ball, and then the sides switch and continue in their new role.

ADAPT:

A: Participants may need to be given hand-over-hand instruction when running bases. Either use colored markers or even use stickers of favorite characters on the markers in order to get the participants familiar and able to recognize the next point to run to.

D: Use larger pylons so the next marker is easier to see.

A: Decrease the space between the bases so that it is easier to move around the bases. Increase space when appropriate.

P: This can be done in a group with other students, but this part of the game may need to be done in a one-on-one setting in order to understand running and being chased to the bases.

T: Use cues and markers appropriate to the interest of the participant or group.

Cool-down: Practice walking the bases at a slower pace but still reinforcing which base is which base. Give arms a big stretch while moving.

Evaluation: Safe? Engaged? Success? Skill development? Is the participant able to move around the bases independently? Without prompting? Do they understand to wait their turn in line or on base?

★ ★ ★
—————————————————— **BONUS** ——————————————————

Catch This

Equipment:

- Balls

Description: One participant has a ball and throws it to their partner. Once the ball is caught the other participant takes a step back and then throws the ball back to their partner. The sequence is repeated, and the first partner takes two steps and the other partner repeats. The number of steps increases each time the ball is caught. If the ball drops the participants start over again.

Adaptations:

- *Simple:* Take out the steps and just throw the ball back and forth. Allow the ball to bounce in between catches.

- *Difficult:* Participants are instructed to throw and catch using only one hand. Instructor can add another ball into the game between the partners.

Softball, Baseball, T-ball

Skills needed: Batting
FMS: Striking, throwing, catching, running

Baseball or Softball Lesson 1

TGfU: Strike or field

Sport: Baseball or softball

FMS: Catching

Skill: Catching

Equipment:

- Funnels
- Soft, small balls
- Gloves
- Two hoops
- Velcro mitts

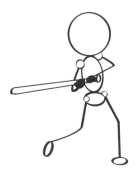

Warm-up: *Mouse catcher.* Give one funnel to each of the participants. The instructor begins rolling balls to the participants, and the participants CATCH the small ball with the funnel and run the ball back to the instructor.

Skill 1: *Big clap catches.* Standing in a circle, participants are shown how to do a big clap with their hands. This can also be called hippo chomps. Use a large, soft ball to throw to the participants, emphasizing catching with a big clap.

Individual or small game: Continue standing in a circle, but change the item to a small ball. Have the participants practice tapping the floor with their fingers, palm facing out. Ensure that each participant is able to get their fingers to tap the ground. The instructor then starts rolling the ball to the participants, emphasizing that they catch the ball with FINGERS DOWN or monkey arms. Emphasize rolling the ball and keeping low to the ground to catch the ball.

Skill 2: *Glove practice.* If there are not enough gloves for each participant, they can also use the Velcro mitts to practice getting used to wearing a glove or something on their hand and starting to catch with one hand and then throwing with the other.

Inclusive game: *Garbage.* Place two hoops about 10 feet apart in the room with at least 10 small balls in each hoop. Each participant has a glove or Velcro mitt and practices catching and throwing the ball back to the other hoop to see who has the most "garbage" left on their side at the end of the game.

ADAPT:

A: Increase or decrease the distance for the participant to catch. Start by rolling, and then move up to throwing.

D: Use a large ball with holes or a Velcro mitt with a tennis ball for easier catching. Use a tennis ball for catching if desired.

A: Keep more or less space between the thrower and the catcher as appropriate.

P: You can start this skill in just a one-on-one environment and move to more people as needed

T: Cueing "glove open" and "eyes watching" when catching. Doing ground ball drills can make it simpler to catch because it is a rolling ball.

Cool-down: Standing in a circle, toss and catch to self a specific number of times.

Evaluation: Safe? Engaged? Success? Skill development? Are they able to catch with a glove? Will they keep the glove on the entire time needed?

Baseball or Softball Lesson 2

TGfU: Strike or field

Sport: Baseball or softball

FMS: Throwing

Skills: Underhand and overhand throwing

Equipment:

- Pylons
- Beanbag
- Bowling pins
- Small playground balls (soft shell) or tennis ball

Warm-up: *Builders and bulldozers.* Scatter various equipment around the space that can be upright or knocked over (pylons, batons, and so on). Divide the class in two groups: *builders*, who try to keep all equipment upright, and *bulldozers*, who try to knock all equipment down. Students should not use their feet or hit equipment with excessive force. Switch roles so all students have the opportunity to play both roles.

Adapted from "Builders and Bulldozers," The Physical Educator, last modified 2017, www.thephysicaleducator.com/game/builders-bulldozers.

Skill 1: Practice giving the high-five motion. Give participants a beanbag or small ball depending on their ability level. Have the participants practice holding the high-five motion with the beanbag or small ball in their hand and then throw the beanbag or small ball against a wall. Back up from the wall as the participant becomes more familiar and comfortable with the motion.

Individual or small game: Set up a tower of pylons, stacking cups, or bowling pins. Have the participants practice overhand throwing in order to knock over the tower of pylons. Repeat if the game is successful.

Skill 2: Underhand throwing. Have the students practice the low-five hand motion with the instructor one-on-one. Then place a beanbag or small ball in their hand, and ask them to throw the beanbag or small ball against a wall. Back up from the wall as the participant becomes more familiar and comfortable with the motion.

Near the end of the activity introduce throwing underhand (low five) and overhand (high five) to see which throw makes the beanbag or ball go the farthest.

Inclusive game: Tape a hoop or item to the wall, or you can lean the hoop against the wall as well, and have the participants throw to hit the target.

ADAPT:

A: Using a sticker on the shoes (for stepping in opposition) to set the footwork pattern alongside the throwing. Use the low- and high-five practice.

D: Use the correct and most comfortable ball that the participant can hold and catch.

A: Decrease or increase the space between the thrower and the catcher.

P: Begin with a one-on-one setting, and then move to group or partner work with a peer.

T: Cue "step, then throw."

Cool-down: Standing in a circle, underhand or overhand throw and catch to self with beanbag.

Evaluation: Safe? Engaged? Success? Skill development? Is there follow-through when throwing? Are they able to differentiate between overhand and underhand and when to use?

Baseball or Softball Lesson 3

TGfU: Strike or field

Sport: Baseball or softball

FMS: Striking

Skill: Batting

Equipment:
- Tall pylons
- Small, soft balls
- Rubber chickens or short pool noodles
- T-ball stand

- Balloons
- Plastic bat

Warm-up: Set up tall pylons with a small ball on top of each pylon. Each participant is given a rubber chicken or a short pool noodle. Have the participants hit as many balls off the pylons as quickly as possible.

Skill 1: Set up a T-ball set if applicable. A large pylon can be used in a pinch. Use a bat, if appropriate, or a rubber chicken to hit a ball off the T-ball stand. Allow a participant to hit three to five times before moving on to the next participant.

Individual or small game: Have the instructor tie balloons to a hockey stick or broom with string. Preferably you would have a couple of instructors for this game to decrease wait times for the participants. Each participant will use the pool noodle or rubber chicken to swing at the balloon.

Skill 2: If appropriate use a plastic bat. Use the T-ball stand again, and have the participants line up and take turns batting and then running the bases. Allow for three swings, and use an appropriate-sized ball. Introduce the idea of "squishing the bug" with the back foot when batting.

Inclusive game: Set up multiple T-ball stands if available. Each participant swings and hits the ball. Once the ball lands, place a beanbag as a marker. See which participant can hit the ball the farthest in the group.

ADAPT:

A: Use a T-ball stand or larger bat when starting batting.

D: Increase the ball size to decrease difficulty. Decrease the ball size when appropriate.

A: Decrease the area where the ball needs to be hit out to.

P: Begin with one-on-one instruction or with a peer partner and then move into a group.

T: Place polyspots or stickers on the ground on both sides of the T-ball stand to remind the participant where to put their feet when batting. Cue "squish the bug" when batting. Cue "elbows up."

Cool-down: Each participant picks up a beanbag and places it in one hand. Cue the student to reach that arm up toward the ceiling for a stretch and then repeat the motion on the other side. Place the beanbag in both hands and reach toward their toes to stretch.

Evaluation: Safe? Engaged? Success? Skill development? Is the hand position correct? Is the motion of swinging correct and smooth?

Baseball or Softball Lesson 4

TGfU: Strike or field

Sport: Baseball or softball

FMS: Running

Skill: Running bases

Equipment:
- Polyspots
- Pylons
- Long skipping rope
- Pinnies
- Bat and ball

Warm-up: Place polyspots all over the space. Allow the participants to move freely around the polyspots.

Skill 1: *Ship to shore (with bases).* Set up a baseball diamond shape in the play area and go over the names of the bases. Give nautical names for the bases, such as "shore" for home base, "ship" for first base, "stern" for second base, and "deck" for third base). Have the participants move around the bases when the instructor calls out the names of the bases.

Adapted from "Ship Shore," Ultimate Camp Resource, accessed December 1, 2022, www.ultimatecampresource.com/camp-games/large-group-games/ship-shore/.

Individual or small game: *Statues.* A small group of students called Statues are on the opposite side of a play space from one student called a Curator. When the Curator turns their back to the Statues, the Statues race across the space to try to tag the Curator. But when the Curator turns around, the Statues must freeze in place and remain frozen as long as the Curator looks at them. The Curator can approach and investigate the Statues, but if their back turns to any of them, the Statues can move toward them. If a Statue is caught moving while the Curator faces them, the Statue has to return to the starting line. The first Statue to tag the Curator becomes the new Curator, and the game repeats.

Variation: Allow the Curator to try to make Statues laugh; any Statue caught laughing has to return to the start line.

Adapted from "Statues at the Museum," PE Central, last modified May 24, 2017, www.pecentral.org/lessonideas/ViewLesson. asp?ID=133201#.YmtkIS971Z0.

Skill 2: Use a long skipping rope or a string. Have two people (instructor and participant) holding either end of the rope. Wiggle the rope right on the ground. The participants take turns in groups of two to three and try to make it over the rope without it touching their feet. This increases their practice of fast feet

Inclusive game: Divide the group into two teams. Pinnies can help with the visual cue of the teams. One team is fielding and catching in the outfield, and the other team is up at bat. Play an adapted game of baseball where extra hits are allowed. Use hand-over-hand instruction. Cue "hit, then drop" (the bat). Stopping or continuing to the next polyspot (base) may take some time and cueing for the participants.

You can cue after "drop" with "one," then "two," then "three," and then "home."

ADAPT:

>**A:** If running consistently needs encouragement, use stickers or items that the participant enjoys to encourage movement.

>**D:** Encourage increasing speed between pylons and bases.

>**A:** Decrease the space between the bases or pylons. Decrease the distance between the pitcher and the batter.

>**P:** Some students may not be comfortable wearing pinnies during a game.

>**T:** Color coordinate the bases from the beginning so that the color gives a visual cue of first, second, or third base.

Cool-down: Each participant picks a base and stands by it (to reinforce where the bases are). Cue the participants to reach both arms ups toward the ceiling and then back down to their toes.

Evaluation: Safe? Engaged? Success? Skill development? Is cueing appropriate and effective? Do the students know the sequence and quickly run the bases?

★ ★ ★
———— **BONUS** ————

Pylon Baseball

Equipment:
- Three pylons for each pair
- Foam balls

Description: Three pylons are set up in a row about five yards apart. A foam ball is placed on top of the middle pylon. Enough stations of pylons are set up so that all the participants are in pairs. One participant (A) stands at one end (home base) of the row of pylons, and another participant (B) stands at the other end. Participant A at the home base pylon walks toward the middle pylon, moves around the middle pylon one time, and then runs back to home base. Participant B at the farthest pylon runs toward the middle pylon once participant A begins to go around the middle pylon. Once participant B reaches the middle pylon with the ball, they pick it up and try to throw the ball and hit home base before their partner does. The ball is to be thrown at the pylon (home base), not at the participant.

Adaptations:
- *Simple:* Decrease the distance between the pylons.
- *Difficult:* The participant at the farthest pylon needs to tag the participant at home base instead of just throwing the ball. Increase the distance between the pylons.

Pylon Base Game

Equipment:
- Four pylons for each group of four
- One ball for each group of four

Description: Have participants make their own baseball field with pylons and divide participants into a group of four (one for each base). Participants practice throwing to each other at different bases. The ball is not allowed to bounce.

Adaptations:
- *Simple:* Participants can roll the ball. Allow two-handed throws and catches. Allow bounces.
- *Difficult:* Participants can throw faster if they are more comfortable.

Belly Baseball Game

Equipment:
- Three large, soft mats
- One Hula-Hoop
- Ball to kick

Description: This game is similar to kickball. Split the group into two teams. One team is in the outfield, and the other team is up to bat. The instructor can be the pitcher for both teams. Use big gym mats or something the students can jump on as first base, second base, and third base. The Hula-Hoop is home base. Review the direction of where the students move throughout the bases and safety around jumping onto the mats.

Have the students each take a base and one in the middle as the pitcher. The other students line up behind home plate. The pitcher rolls the ball slowly or quickly toward the batter. The batter kicks the ball, and then the other outfielders try to pick up the kicked ball as quickly as possible as the batter moves around the bases. This is continued until all the batters have had a chance to kick the ball, and then the sides switch.

Adaptations:
- *Simple:* Allow more than one child to stop on a base. Outfielders only need to have the ball under control for the runner to have to stop. The instructor can allow for more time needed, depending on the ability level of the students to move.
- *Difficult:* Play with a Nerf ball and bat.

Invasion Games

The goal of invasion games is to control an object, keep the object away from opponents, and move the object into a scoring position in order to attack a goal. Offensive and defensive participants share the same space and try to prevent the other participants from scoring. Lesson plans for soccer, basketball, floor hockey, and American football are provided. Bonus games are included.

Soccer

Skills needed: Dribbling, shooting, passing, trapping
FMS: Running, kicking, trapping

Soccer Lesson 1

TGfU: Invasion

Sport: Soccer

FMS: Running, kicking

Skill: Dribbling

Equipment:
- Pinnies
- Soccer balls (or other balls)
- Red and green beanbags or polyspots
- Pylons

Warm-up: Monkeys and baboons. The instructor explains the difference between monkeys and baboons. A monkey has a tail and a baboon does not. The leader will give two to four participants (depending on the size of the group) pinnies to put in their pants pocket, which will show the rest of the participants that they are the monkeys. The other participants will not have pinnies, and they will be the baboons. The leader explains that the baboons want a tail and will try to steal the tail from the monkeys (*Alberta Soccer, 2018*).

Skill 1: Each participant has a soccer ball. Define an area with lines or pylons. Students can move in any direction with the ball at their feet. Give cues such as "use right foot," "use left foot," and "keep ball close."

Individual or small game: *Red light, green light (with ball)*. Have the participants move the ball with their feet while one student acts as a traffic light, calling out the traffic colors. Yellow can be used in order move slowly with the ball.

Skill 2: Line up eight pylons in a row on one side, and then have about two feet in between another eight pylons and have the participants move slowly (or to their ability pace), moving the ball in between the pylons. Make the space in between the pylon row smaller each time to force more control on the ball. Cue using "big toe" contact around the inside of the pylon and "Little toe" to cross back around the pylon.

Inclusive game: Use pylons to mark off the playing area. One participant is chosen to stand in the middle of the playing space (or the instructor can be in this position). The chosen participant can move freely in the space and does not have a ball. All of the other participants have one ball. All but the middle person, are lined up on one side of the playing space. The goal is to move from one side of the playing area to the other side, moving around and away from the chosen participant and not losing control of their ball. If a participant is tagged or loses their ball, they join the chosen participant in the middle and try to tag the remaining participants.

ADAPT:

A: Using a beanbag instead of a ball may allow for more control on a floor. Use a ball that is an appropriate size and speed for the participant. A soccer ball is not necessary. Color can help encourage a choice from the participant.

D: Decrease the speed of ball movement by encouraging a slower speed of the game.

A:. Create an area outside the pylons that is considered the safe zone where participants cannot be tagged. This can be used if a participant becomes anxious. Determine a maximum amount of time that a participant can be in the safe zone.

P: Start in a one-on-one or peer-partner setting. Move to group work when appropriate.

T: Allow the participants to move freely and independently with the ball. A sticker or a timer can help keep the participant engaged with the ball.

Cool-down: With the soccer ball in hands, stretch up toward the ceiling and then down to the floor.

Evaluation: Safe? Engaged? Success? Skill development? Is the participant able to control the movement of the ball? With dominant foot? With nondominant foot?

Soccer Lesson 2

TGfU: Invasion

Sport: Soccer

FMS: Receiving

Skill: Trapping

Equipment:

- Beanbags
- Soccer ball (other balls)

Warm-up: Have the participants move around the space kicking a beanbag and stomping on it with their foot. Emphasize the squish.

Skill 1: Have the participants move freely around the room with a soccer ball. On the command from the instructor call out to "Squish the ball," where the participants will stop and squish the ball with the insides of both of their feet.

Individual or small game: Participants will practice stopping or trapping the ball with either one or two feet and then kicking it either back to a wall or to another participant.

Skill 2: Groups of three. One person holds onto a Hula-Hoop with one student on each side of the hoop. One student kicks the soccer ball through the hoop, and the third student traps the ball on the other side. This trapping is to present the receiving foot in line with the ball, then relax it on contact. Reverse direction several times and change roles.

Inclusive game: Make a circle with all of the participants. Place two pylons about three feet apart in the middle of the circle. Have students kick and trap the ball back and forth to each other while trying to put it through the pylon goal. Count how many times the ball stays inside the circle or count the number of goals.

ADAPT:

A: Start with a beanbag, and then move on to a ball for more control.

D: Going outside on the grass (rather than using the gym floor) will slow the ball down.

A: Decrease the distance that the participant needs to travel with the ball.

P: Begin with a one-on-one session or with a peer partner. Move into a small group of four or more when appropriate.

T: Try to do this session in a smaller room so that the balls are not distracting and rolling around all over the place. Cue with "squish" to keep the ball close to the participant.

Cool-down: Participants take their soccer ball and reach it up over their head. They then place it down on the floor, reach down to the floor, place their hands on the ball, and stretch down to their feet.

Evaluation: Safe? Engaged? Success? Skill development? Does the student line up their body with the incoming ball?

Soccer Lesson 3

TGfU: Invasion

Sport: Soccer

FMS: Kicking

Skills: Shooting and passing

Equipment:
- Pylons
- Soccer balls (other balls okay)

Warm-up: Place pylons around the space. The instructor tells the participants that they need to kick the pylons down as quickly as possible. Emphasize using the laces, meaning the contact point should be where their laces are on their shoe rather than kicking with their toes.

Skill 1: *Shooting.* Line participants up by the wall, and have the participants kick the ball toward the wall as hard as they can. Place the support foot beside the ball. Swing the kicking leg back, bend the knee to bring it over the ball, extend the bottom of the leg, and strike with the laces in the middle of the ball.

Individual or small game: *Coconuts.* Make a line of soccer balls sitting on pylons in the middle of the space. Divide the group with half on one side of the ball line and half on the other side. Participants on the outside also each have a ball. The participants dribble forward once and then kick their ball to try and knock the balls off the pylons. If a ball is knocked off, safely bring the ball to their side. Keep playing continuously. The team that knocks the most balls off wins (*Alberta Soccer,* 2018).

Skill 2: *Passing.* Participants pair off and then kick one ball back and forth in a line. Practice standing on one foot, open hip, swinging kicking leg with toe pointing up, and contacting the ball with the side of the foot. Ask players to move and continue to pass to each other.

Inclusive game: *One-on-one.* Partners each with the two same-colored pylons. Make a goal with the pylons one giant step apart. One ball per pair. The participants try to score on their partner. If they score, the ball is given to the other participant. This can progress to two-on-two.

ADAPT:

A: Change the ball size and use a utility ball.

D: Emphasize the stepping in opposition (sticker) in order to kick the ball.

A: Use a ball appropriate and encouraging enough for the participant.

P: Begin one-on-one or with a peer partner. Move to three to four participants and then into a large group.

T: Use the cue "step and kick" to emphasize using the correct foot. Using the idea of a dinosaur foot (use a dinosaur sticker), which is the foot the participant kicks with, will help emphasize a big kick and the correct foot to use.

Cool-down: Walk around the area and pick up the pylons. Who can get the most back to the teacher?

Evaluation: Safe? Engaged? Success? Skill development? Is the participant able to control the effort and speed of the ball when shooting?

Soccer Lesson 4

TGfU: Invasion

Sport: Soccer

FMS: Running, shooting, catching

Skills: Game play or goalie

Equipment:

- Pinnies
- Soccer balls (other balls)
- Pylons or nets

Warm-up: *Monkeys and baboons.* The instructor explains the difference between monkeys and baboons. A monkey has a tail and a baboon does not. The leader will give two to four participants (depending on the size of the group) pinnies to put in their pants pocket, which will show the rest of the participants that they are the monkeys. The other participants will not have pinnies, and they will be the baboons. The leader explains that the baboons want a tail and will try to steal the tail from the monkey.

Adapted by permission from "Donkey Tails," Alberta Soccer Association, Grassroots Session Toolkit, accessed December 1, 2022, www.albertasoccer.com/wp-content/uploads/2018/01/GrassrootsSessionsToolkitFINAL.pdf.

Skill 1: Practice holding hands out in front. Have the instructor throw the ball to the participants, and they will catch it with two hands and pull it to their chest. Then the participant throws the ball back to the instructor using "Elbows up" and a two-hand overhand throw.

Individual or small game: *Soccer relay race.* Participants dribble the ball through the pylons, and then they take a shot on a net. Walk through the pattern first. Return to start. Count number of goals.

Skill 2: Set up two to four nets and divide the group into small groups between the nets. Rotate the participants so everyone gets a turn to be in the goalie position and in the shooting position. Encourage goalies to be "big like a gorilla," with arms outstretched and hands facing the shooter.

Inclusive game: *Three-on-three.* One is a goalie. Partners have the two same-colored pylons. Make a goal with the pylons one giant step apart. One ball per pair. The participants try to score. If they score, the ball is given to the other participant. Rotate positions so everyone plays goalie.

ADAPT:

A: Keeping the ball low and slow when starting out can help ease any anxieties the participant may feel.

D: Use a lighter, bigger ball, which is easier to catch.

A: Increase the distance the kicker has to the net to make it more difficult for the kicker but easier for the goalie.

P: Use a bigger group, but use more nets so that the number of kickers is less with each goalie, and everyone gets a turn.

T: Use the cues "Hands up" and "Eyes up."

Cool-down: Walk and pick up pylons. How many can you return?

Evaluation: Safe? Engaged? Success? Skill development? Was the game play successful? Were the goalies able to catch most of the shots?

BONUS

Shark Attack

Equipment:
- Pylons to specify two lines
- Soccer balls

Description: Make two lines of players 30 to 40 feet apart. At one end is the ocean, and the other is the safe coral reef. One line are sharks at the ocean. One line with soccer balls are fish coming from the coral reef. Fish try to get to the ocean without the sharks stealing their ball. The leader can say "shark attack" to release the sharks. Fish can try to make the ocean or return to the coral reef. If a fish loses the ball, they become a shark.

Adaptations:
- *Simple:* Reduce the number of sharks. Sharks must walk. Sharks only touch the ball rather than gain possession.
- *Difficult:* Reduce the space between the two lines of players so the fish don't have as much space to move away from the shark.

Four-Goal Game

Equipment:
- Eight pylons or four small goals
- Soccer balls

Description: Split the group into two teams and have four nets instead of two, which allows for more turns for students to be the goalie as well as more shooting opportunities for the rest of the group. One could also add another ball to allow more ball time per student.

Adaptations:

- *Simple:* Use a big ball instead of a soccer ball. Reduce the number of players. Slow the pace to walking. Reduce the playing area. Allow students to touch the ball with their hands.
- *Difficult:* Increase the playing area.

Basketball

Skills needed: Dribbling, shooting, passing
FMS: Throwing, catching

Basketball Lesson 1

TGfU: Invasion

Sport: Basketball

FMS: Throwing

Skill: Dribbling

Equipment:

- Basketballs (other balls okay)
- Red and green beanbags
- Polyspots
- Pylons

Warm-up: In a circle, have all of the participants throw and catch a ball any way they want to do it. Call out a name before throwing, then add in a bounce to one-self, and then throw to someone else.

Skill 1: Have the participants sit in a circle. Each participant has a ball. Basketballs are optional but it needs to be a ball that bounces. Start with bouncing the ball with two hands, either between the legs or in front of the legs. If that is mastered, move up to bouncing it with two hands in a kneeling position. Attempt one-hand bounces. Then move on to standing and either bouncing with two hands or dribbling with one hand. The participant can move between these levels as needed.

Individual or small game: Play red light, green light, but with a basketball. One participant is the traffic light and calls the color of the light ("red" to stop, "green" to go fast, and "yellow" to go slow) and the rest of the group are dribbling their basketballs and moving around the space. The objective of the game is to keep control of the basketball while changing the pace.

Adapted from "Red Light, Green Light," Playworks, accessed December 21, 2022, www.playworks.org/game-library/red-light-green-light.

Skill 2: *Bubble breakers.* Polyspots are randomly placed around the gym or room. Participants move around the room trying to dribble on the most polyspots in the allotted time.

Inclusive game: *Dribbling relay race.* Line the students up behind an allotted space with pylons or polyspots. Each participant dribbles the ball or two-hand bounces to the allotted item and then back to the group as quickly as possible.

ADAPT:

 A: Try a ball that bounces and not a basketball if it is too hard.

 D: Use an appropriate and comfortable-size ball for the participant to be able to dribble comfortably and with success.

 A: Decrease the vertical space between the participant and the floor so that it is easier to catch and control.

 P: One-on-one play is the easiest for most skills in basketball, and then move to peer partners.

 T: Like in the soccer unit, red light, green light is a great game to play when learning a dribbling skill because it slows things down and makes it fun.

Cool-down: Each participant has a basketball or ball. With that ball the participants can reach up to the ceiling, twist side to side, and reach down to their toes.

Evaluation: Safe? Engaged? Success? Skill development? Is control of the ball being maintained? Are the hand pressure and position correct?

Basketball Lesson 2

TGfU: Invasion

Sport: Basketball

FMS: Throwing

Skill: Passing

Equipment:

 • Basketball (other balls okay)

 • Hula-Hoop

Warm-up: Place Hula-Hoops all around the space. Have the participants move freely in the space. When the instructor calls out "Find a hoop," each participant steps into a hoop. Work on moving fast and slow.

Skill 1: Bounce pass. Practice dropping the ball to another participant back and forth. Keep bounces short and clean. Pairs should be close together so that it is easier to catch.

Individual or small game: Line up all of the participants in a straight line. Practice walking all together, side by side, back and forth in the space. Then add a ball into the line, passing the ball to everyone in line in order while still walking. Using cues and watching for your neighbor to pass the ball will help in an actual game.

Skill 2: Chest pass. Practice with a wall or an instructor, and practice throwing the ball from the chest to the wall. Teach elbows out, passing to the chest, from the chest, fingers apart, flicking wrist, and legs shoulder width apart.

Inclusive game: Participants stand in a circle as a group. First practice sending bounce passes to each other, and then take a step back to practice chest passes.

ADAPT:

A: Take out the dribbling portion of the game in order to decrease the skill level.

D: Use a ball appropriate for the participant's size, age, and ability.

A: Keep participants closer together during the game so that they don't have to pass as far. Or do the activity seated.

P: One-on-one instruction works well, but a larger group can work well if the ball is appropriate for all participants.

T: Walking together is harder than it looks! Keeping pace with everyone requires attention.

Cool-down: Standing in a circle, the participants reach their hands up toward the ceiling then down to their toes.

Evaluation: Safe? Engaged? Success? Skill development? Is the bounce pass and chest pass executed with appropriate weight and direction?

Basketball Lesson 3

TGfU: Invasion

Sport: Basketball

FMS: Throwing

Skill: Shooting

Equipment:

- Basketball (other balls okay)
- Hula-Hoops
- Basketball net
- Tape or marking on the wall

Warm-up: *Wall tag.* Have the participants move around the space. The instructor calls out and gives a visual cue where the participants give a high five to the wall. Move around the room and ensure that the hand reaches up as high as it would in a shot.

Skill 1: Practice shooting a ball to a marked spot on the wall. Use a lighter ball to start, and then with practice one can move to a basketball.

Individual or small game: If the area has multiple hoops, the participants can move to a variety of hoops and attempt to shoot on them. If not possible, have the participants throw into a Hula-Hoop being held by the instructor.

Skill 2: Place Hula-Hoops on the floor in front of a basketball net. Have the students place the hoops where they think they can shoot the best. Have the participants shoot from there and see if it works. Ask questions and move around to see which spot is the most comfortable for each participant.

Skill development: Layups can also be practiced by placing three sticky mats in a curved pattern alongside a line on the basketball court. Participants take three steps, then are cued to hop and shoot the basketball toward the net with one hand.

Inclusion game: Basketball game. Use lower nets or Hula-Hoops tied to the baskets with skipping ropes. Use pinnies and encourage walking and sharing the ball.

ADAPT:

A: Keep the skill the main focus and not actually achieving success in shooting. Target and follow-through are important to practice.

D: Lower the hoop height, or use a lighter ball.

A: Allow for shots to be taken to be closer to the net than traditionally allowed. With practice, have the participant move back to increase difficulty.

P: This can be done individually, or if multiple nets are available a larger group can be used.

T: Allow two-handed dribbles, disregard the three-second rule violation, and slow the pace by walking during a game.

Cool-down: Each participant will have a pinny. Have the participants take the pinnies off and use them to stretch. Grab the pinny with both hands and reach up toward the ceiling with straight arms. Keeping arms straight, tilt to the sides and then forward, down to their toes.

Evaluation: Safe? Engaged? Success? Skill development? Shooting accuracy? Hand position correct on ball when shooting?

⭐⭐⭐
——————— **BONUS** ———————

Can't Touch It!

Equipment:
- Soft ball
- Two net goals

Description: Participants are divided into two teams. Pinnies can be used as a visual cue for teams. This game is similar to handball because each team is trying to get the ball into the opposing team's net. Nets are set up at each end of the playing area. Goalies can be used, depending on the ability and number of participants.

Each team is allowed three passes within their own team before the opposing team can attempt to intercept and steal the ball. Once intercepted the ball goes to that team for a minimum of three throws, and then, once again, the ball can be intercepted and stolen by the other team.

These rules allow the game play to be slowed down and for everyone on each team to get a chance to play.

Adaptations:

- *Simple:* All participants use their hands to catch and throw the ball. Have all the team members count the number of passes out loud.
- *Difficult:* Add a pylon or tub at each end of the playing area so that teams can score bonus points after the successful three to five passes.

Hot Shots

Equipment:

- Polyspots
- Hula-Hoops
- Basketballs

Description: Place polyspots randomly near the basketball hoops, and have Hula-Hoops hanging from basketball net. If a student shoots from the polyspot, then they get to pick up the spot and take it to the teacher. The goal is to collect spots.

Adaptations:

- *Simple:* Spots are placed close to the hoops. Allow one step from the spot to count.
- *Difficult:* Spots are placed farther away from the hoops.

Floor Hockey

Skills needed: Stick handling, shooting, running with a stick
FMS: Striking

Floor Hockey Lesson 1

TGfU: Invasion

Sport: Floor hockey or ringette

FMS: Striking

Skill: Shooting

Equipment:

- Hockey or ringette stick
- Hula-Hoop
- Beanbags

Warm-up: Each participant stands in a hoop holding a hockey stick or ringette stick. Each hoop has a minimum of 10 beanbags. Line up the participants in a row or in a circle, and instruct the participants to shoot the beanbags out as far as they can. You can have a target or see who can get it the farthest or closest.

Skill 1: Place tape or sticky notes on a wall in the space. Have the participants spread out and try to shoot the targets on the wall with precision.

Individual or small game: Break up the participants into two teams or two groups, where half of the participants are near the nets and the other half are shooting. Use a light foam ball or beanbag, and practice shooting on the net. The instructor is in the net to reduce the chances for participant injury.

Skill 2: Wrist shot practice. Have the participants stand on two lines on the floor or use the Hula-Hoop. Demonstrate how to drag a beanbag or puck back between the lines with their feet on the front line or in front of the Hula-Hoop. Feet stay in position, but the stick moves the beanbag back slightly and then follows through to push the beanbag or puck farther ahead.

Inclusive game: Set up a series of pylons or a net, and have the participants move from net to net attempting to shoot the beanbag or puck into the net successfully or after a certain number of shots and move on to the next.

ADAPT:

A: Use an appropriate target or item to shoot. It is very important that the implement is the correct height for the participant.

D: A larger light ball or balloon can be used instead of a puck or beanbag.

A: A larger space with a smooth floor or an outdoor area is better than a carpeted area. Use a small ball if in a carpeted area, but it will be a bit harder to control.

P: One-on-one play is good to begin with and is safer with the stick, but this can also be done as a group.

T: Cue the participant to give a "big push" to the beanbag or puck.

Cool-down: Have the participants use their sticks to push all of the beanbags back into the storage bins. Then use the stick to lean on to do a calf stretch on both sides.

Evaluation: Safe? Engaged? Success? Skill development?

Shooting for accuracy with power?

Floor Hockey Lesson 2

TGfU: Invasion

Sport: Floor hockey or ringette

FMS: Dodging, trapping

Skill: Stick handling

Equipment:

- Hockey or ringette stick
- Beanbags
- Pucks
- Pylons
- Hula-Hoops

Warm-up: Each participant has a hockey or ringette stick. Have the participants move around the space with their stick. One participant is the tagger and tries to tag other participants' sticks with their own stick. Sticks need to be kept on the ground. Once tagged, that participant is the tagger.

Skill 1: Give each participant a stick and a beanbag. Pylons are set up randomly around the room. Have the participant move freely with their stick and beanbag around the space, but they have to keep their beanbag with them the whole time. They can move around the pylons with their stick and beanbag. Putting a fun sticker on the beanbag or using animal beanbags can help keep them interested.

Individual or small game: *Treasure chest.* Two hoops are set up at opposite sides of the playing area. The hoops are different colors to distinguish teams. Beanbags are divided equally between the hoops. Participants are divided into two teams. These two teams each have their own hoop. The beanbags are considered their "treasure." The point of the game is to steal the other team's beanbags in a given amount of time, moving the beanbags with their sticks (Physed Games, 2022).

Skill 2: *Stick handling relay race.* Set up a pylon a distance away from the participants. The participant moves the beanbag up and around the pylon and back before the next person goes. You can split this game up into more groups to allow for more play time and less waiting around. Advance to a small ball.

Inclusive game: *Ollie, ollie, octopus.* Each participant is given a stick and beanbag. Participants line up on one side of the playing area. The leader will stand in the middle of the room. Once the leader gives the verbal cue "ollie, ollie, octopus" the participants travel while keeping control of their bean bag with their stick, from one side of the room to the other without being tagged by the leader (the octopus). If tagged, the participant stops where they are, puts down their stick, and tries to tag other participants with their hands. The game is played until only one participant is left. The last person becomes the new octopus.

Adapted from "Ollie Ollie Octopus," Fit Kids Healthy Kids, accessed December 1, 2022, https://fkhk.sportmanitoba.ca/node/697.

ADAPT:

A: The correct height and weight of the stick are necessary for comfort and ease of the skills. Pool noodles can be used.

D: Use an appropriate item to shoot with, either a large, light ball or something that cannot hurt, such as a foam ball or beanbag.

A: Use an area with a smooth floor surface and ample space to move the stick. Reduce the space if the object of the game cannot be accomplished.

P: One-on-one setting or a small group. This skill is a bit slower so a larger group is okay too.

T: Encouraging proper beanbag or puck control over speed is important as well as keeping the stick *on the ground* to avoid injury.

Cool-down: Students clean up the beanbags by pushing the beanbags back to the storage bin. Students raise their sticks to the sky, bend side to side holding the stick, and bring the stick to their toes.

Evaluation: Safe? Engaged? Success? Skill development? Are the students able to keep the beanbag or ball in control on their stick?

Floor Hockey Lesson 3

TGfU: Invasion

Sport: Floor hockey or ringette

FMS: Dribbling, trapping

Skill: Blocking

Equipment:

- Hockey or ringette sticks
- Beanbags
- Pylons
- Balloons

Warm-up: *Monkeys and baboons.* This game is a great way to get the participants moving and chasing each other, which is needed for game play in hockey and ringette. Explain the difference between monkeys and baboons. A monkey has a tail, and a baboon does not. The leader will give two to four participants (depending on the size of the group) pinnies to put in their pants pocket, which will show the rest of the participants that they are the monkeys. The other participants will not have pinnies, and they will be called the baboons. The leader explains that the baboons want a tail and will try to steal the tail from the monkeys.

Adapted by permission from "Donkey Tails," Alberta Soccer Association, Grassroots Session Toolkit, accessed December 1, 2022, www.albertasoccer.com/wp-content/uploads/2018/01/GrassrootsSessionsToolkitFINAL.pdf.

Skill 1: Give each participant a stick and have the instructor either shoot at them or break them into pairs. The shooter hits a balloon to the student, and the student tries to stop the balloon with their hand or their stick.

Individual or small game: Have all of the participants stand in a circle with their hands up. Pass the balloon back and forth with either their hands or their feet. Try to speed up the pace of moving the balloon in the circle without it stopping.

Skill 2: Move back to skill 1. Change out the balloon for either a foam ball or a beanbag. The participant can use a baseball glove on their nonstick hand if comfortable and try blocking shots from either other participants or the instructor. Ensure that the shots are slow and numbered so that the participant knows what is coming.

Inclusive game: One participant has a beanbag or puck and the rest of the group stands on the other side of this participant. The participant takes a shot toward the group, and the group tries to block the shot. They can have sticks with the beanbags, or you can use a balloon, and the group of participants just use their hands. This game can be done with the participants and a helper or two participants together, alternating the roles.

ADAPT:

A: Use a slower pace when shooting by having a larger, lighter ball to shoot so that the participant blocking has more time to react.

D: Give more distance between the shooter and the goalie.

A: Use an area with ample space to move with a stick, and the flooring should be smooth enough for players to move the beanbag or puck.

P: One-on-one instruction may be more comfortable to start with blocking. It can be harder to learn if the participant is nervous, so use one-on-one instruction until they are more comfortable with a peer.

T: Cueing "Stick on the ground" to avoid high shots near a participant's head is important when first starting. If participants are comfortable, you can allow the beanbags and pucks to get air.

Cool-down: Participants use their sticks to balance, stand on one foot, and stretch both quadriceps.

Evaluation: Safe? Engaged? Success? Skill development? Are the students able to block objects coming toward their bodies?

BONUS

Link Ball Pass

Equipment:
- Two sets of colored pinnies or bibs
- Soft balls

Description: Divide the participants into two teams, and then give both teams different-colored pinnies. Next, all the participants stand in a circle, alternating positions in the circle between each team. Participants then put their feet about shoulder width apart with the outside of their foot against their neighbor's foot. Use a soft ball for the game. Participants will try to hit the ball with their hand between the legs of an opposing team member. Participants' feet must stay in contact the entire game. Participants defend their goal by hitting the ball away. A ball is not allowed to be caught and can only be struck by hands.

Adaptations:
- *Simple:* Allow the ball to be caught with both hands. Participants can also sit down and open their legs (to act as a goal) and play the game on the floor.
- *Difficult:* Add multiple balls into the game.

Hockey Obstacle Course

Equipment:
- Pylons or other obstacles
- Ball or pucks
- Sticks

Description: Participants practice stick handling by setting up an obstacle course beforehand and working together as a team to get all their teammates through the obstacles as quickly as possible.

Adaptations:
- *Simple:* Set up a row of pylons and have participant move the hockey puck through the pylons.
- *Difficult:* Space the pylons closer together.

Ready, Go, Stop

Equipment:

- Sticks

Description: Have the students practice moving around the space with a hockey stick. Yell "Go" and "Stop" to start and stop. To increase skill, show the proper ready position for floor hockey, and have the students get into that position when stopping.

Adaptations:

- *Simple:* Walking only. No sticks.
- *Difficult:* Add balls, beanbags, or pucks.

Boomerang Shooting Game

Equipment:

- Sticks
- Pucks or balls

Description: Set up two nets in close proximity to each other and have the students take turns shooting on one net and then running back and shooting on the other net as quickly as they can. No goalies are needed, but they can be added in. Students will have to move around their classmates quickly while keeping their puck close to them.

Adaptations:

- *Simple:* Reduce the distance between the nets. Increase the size of the nets. Allow walking only.
- *Difficult:* Set a time, and count how many in the set time. Do several rounds to try and beat own score.

Football

Skills needed: Overhand throwing, catching, kicking
FMS: Running, throwing, catching, kicking

Football Lesson 1

TGfU: Invasion

Sport: Football

FMS: Throwing, catching

Skills: Overhand throwing, catching

Equipment:
- Hula-Hoop
- Football (foam preferred)
- Rubber chicken
- Polyspot

Warm-up: Find a hoop. Participants move freely around the space while Hula-Hoops are on the floor in a random pattern. When the instructor calls "Find a hoop" all the participants must go and find a Hula-Hoop to stand in.

Skill 1: Find a hoop and throw. Participants continue with the warm-up game, but this time a ball or a football is added into the game. Once the participants are in a hoop, the instructor can throw to any participants who are standing in a hoop. If they are not standing in a hoop they cannot be thrown to. Then allow the participants to move around again, and again call out "Find a hoop" and then throw to participants whose hands are ready to catch.

Individual or small game: Use a rubber chicken for each participant. Have the participants put the chicken into their dominant hand, and instruct the participants to move around the space and smack the rubber chicken against various walls and surfaces in the room. Cue "elbow up" and emphasize the *smack* sound.

Skill 2: Place a polyspot in front of each participant, and reinforce the pattern of stepping in opposition before throwing. Then add in the rubber chicken–throwing movement. Cue "step, then throw."

Inclusive game: If you place the participants in front of a wall, you can create a challenge to see who can get the chicken the highest on the wall or the lowest on the wall or the loudest.

ADAPT:
   A: Rubber gloves can be substituted in for rubber chickens.

   D: If the glove or chicken is too easy, add in a football instead to get the feel of the weight needed.

   A: Decrease or increase the space between the thrower and the catcher.

   P: Peer partners or groups of partners can start off together and then go into small teams.

   T: Allow for stepping in opposition to be introduced from an earlier session. Stickers can be used to reinforce a visual cue.

Cool-down: Holding the rubber chicken in both hands, reach up toward the ceiling and stretch arms over the head. Then have the participants reach down toward their toes.

Evaluation: Safe? Engaged? Success? Skill development? Is there follow-through with the arm? Is stepping in opposition automatic?

Football Lesson 2

TGfU: Invasion

Sport: Football

FMS: Catching

Skill: Football catch

Equipment:

- Beach ball or big light ball
- Small foam balls
- Foam footballs
- Buckets or containers

Warm-up: Sitting in a circle or standing, practice catching with "hippo chomps." Use a beach ball or a larger ball for more fun.

Skill 1: Using a soft ball, have the participants practice squishing the ball with various parts of their body. Emphasize the squishing with the arms and stomach area. Show the air coming in and out of the ball.

Individual or small game: Practice with a partner throwing and squishing the air out of the ball when catching. Who can make the ball the smallest?

Skill 2: Participants can try with a foam football, passing it back and forth with a partner or in a circle.

Inclusive game: Using buckets or plastic containers, have the instructor throw a light, soft ball high in the air and have the participants attempt to catch it with their bucket.

ADAPT:

A: Foam footballs can give participants the feel of the ball without the weight.

D: Decrease the space or increase the space between the catcher and the thrower.

A: Smaller contained areas are easier to catch footballs in than a wide open space.

P: One-on-one or peer partners to start and improve skills.

T: Squishing and hippo chomps are used in other sports.

Cool-down: Have the participants stack the buckets together. Then taking both hands reach up toward the ceiling and stretch. Then reach the hands back down to the toes and stretch.

Evaluation: Safe? Engaged? Success? Skill development? Do the hands and arms come in to catch?

Football Lesson 3

TGfU: Invasion

Sport: Football

FMS: Kicking

Skills: Dropkick and punting

Equipment:
- Pylons
- Rubber chicken or glove
- Pylon
- Basket or bucket
- Beanbags
- Footballs

Warm-up: *Builders and bulldozers.* Scatter various equipment around the space that can be upright or knocked over (pylons, batons, and so on). Divide the class in two groups: *builders*, who try to keep all equipment upright, and *bulldozers*, who try to knock all equipment down. Students should not use their feet or hit equipment with excessive force. Switch roles so all students have the opportunity to play both roles.

Adapted from "Builders and Bulldozers," The Physical Educator, last modified 2017, www.thephysicaleducator.com/game/builders-bulldozers.

Skill 1: Each participant is given a rubber chicken or a rubber glove. Have the participant hold the object with both hands in front of them, bending slightly at the waist, and instruct the participant to kick the item. Aim to contact the widest part of the object with the top of their foot.

Individual or small game: Place the chicken on the top of the pylon. Use one pylon per participant, or you can make a line. Have the participant kick the chicken off the top of the pylon. The goal is to see how high you can get the chicken to "fly."

Skill 2: On low pylons, place an upright football and have the participants kick the football off of the low pylon.

Inclusive game: Place beanbags all over the area and a basket or bucket nearby. The goal is to have one team kicking the ball while the other team is trying to clean up as many beanbags as they can before the ball hits the ground.

ADAPT:

A: Use rubber gloves instead of a rubber chicken.

D: Use a larger item to kick so it's easier, or have the instructor help hold the chicken or rubber glove to make it easier.

A: Use an indoor space to decrease the amount of running to get the ball, as opposed to an outdoor space.

P: Use peer partners or a small group doing individual skills.

T: Cue "step, then kick" (as in soccer), and use a sticker if that helps with a visual cue.

Cool-down: Participants clean up the beanbags and put them back into the storage bin as quickly as possible. Each participant reaches up toward the ceiling and then back down toward their toes.

Evaluation: Safe? Engaged? Success? Skill development? Is balance maintained while kicking? Is the foot able to point upward?

Football Lesson 4

TGfU: Invasion

Sport: Football

FMS: Running, throwing, catching

Skill: Game play

Equipment:

- Pinnies
- Footballs (foam if needed)
- Polyspots
- Hula-Hoops

Warm-up: *Pinny tag.* One to two participants use a pinny to tag other participants who don't have a pinny. Once caught they are given the pinny, and they become the tagger.

Skill 1: In a circle, participants pass the ball in a circle. Start to vary the size of the circle. Do five throws or passes, and then either increase or decrease the circle.

Individual or small game: *Ollie ollie octopus.* Participants move around the room trying not to get tagged by the octopus. If caught, the participant then becomes an octopus.

Adapted from "Ollie Ollie Octopus," Fit Kids Healthy Kids, accessed December 1, 2022, https://fkhk.sportmanitoba.ca/node/697.

Skill 2: *Obstacle course.* Have the group or instructor set up an obstacle course around the space with various objects like pylons or polyspots and footballs. Have the participants move around the course as quickly as they can to work on quick feet and turns.

Inclusive game: Place polyspots or Hula-Hoops around the space and have the students start at one end of the room. Divide the students into two teams with pinnies. One team starts with the ball (can be a football) and then passes to anyone else on their team who is standing on a polyspot. The other team can try to stop the ball from being caught, and then they go onto the polyspots.

ADAPT:

A: Encourage a chasing or tagging environment so that game play in football comes easier.

D: Slow down the speed of the game if the participant isn't able to keep up by walking.

A: Decrease or increase the space or speed of the game played as needed.

P: Using a number of participants makes this more complicated but is necessary to give a real feel for the game of football.

T: This game method just slows down the game so that everyone is able to see what is going on.

Cool-down: Participants clean up as many polyspots as they can and stack them on the side of the room. With the pinny in both hands the participant reaches up toward the ceiling and then back down toward their toes.

Evaluation: Safe? Engaged? Success? Skill development? Are the students understanding invading the opponent's space?

Warm-Up and Sport Skill Games

The next section includes warm-up and sport skill games that can be used with any TGfU game form.

Warm-Up Games

Fitness Dice

Equipment: One die with various fitness activities on it (eight in total) and a die with various numbers on it.

Description: Participants take turns rolling the dice and completing the activities as a group.

Adaptations:

- *Simple*: Leader rolls both dice and instructs participants.
- *Difficult*: Participants break into small groups and take turns rolling and calling out the activities and numbers.

Line Tag

Equipment: Pinnies or bibs

Description: Participants spread out in the playing area, preferably in a gymnasium where there are lines on the floor, but if not you can use masking tape on the floor. Participants are instructed that they must stay on the lines. This can be practiced before playing the game. Participants can walk, run, or use any locomotor skill to move around the space. One or two participants (or the leaders) try to tag other participants. Once tagged, the participant becomes it and must try to tag someone else. Pinnies can be used in order to show who is it, with it carrying the pinny in their hand.

Adapted from K. Boulton, "Line Tag," Elementary P.E. Games, accessed December 1, 2022, www.elementarypegames.weebly.com/line-tag.html.

Adaptations:

- *Simple:* Use only half of the space because it makes less space for participants to cover. Participants can walk instead of run.
- *Difficult:* Running is used. Increase the playing area. Add more participants that are taggers.

Pylon to Ball (Ship to Shore)

Equipment: Ball, pylon

Description: Place a ball on one side of the room and a pylon on the opposite side of the room. Instruct participants to move to either the ball or the pylon. Allow enough transition time before calling out a new location.

Adapted from "Ship Shore," Ultimate Camp Resource, accessed December 1, 2022, www.ultimatecampresource.com/camp-games/large-group-games/ship-shore/.

Adaptations:

- *Simple:* Walk between objects. Place items closer together so less distance is traveled.
- *Difficult:* Running or add a more difficult locomotor skill (crab walking, skipping). Place objects farther apart. Instructions can be called out quicker, with less transition time in between, thus allowing for quick direction changes.

4 Wall Run

Equipment: None

Description: Designate four walls in the playing area. Have participants point and say the number out loud with the leader. Once the participants are comfortable with the four walls, the game can begin. Leader yells out a number (1, 2, 3, 4), and the participants run as fast as they can to that wall.

Adaptations:

- *Simple:* Participants can walk instead of run.
- *Difficult:* Call out the numbers more quickly with shorter transition times.

Sharks and Sailors

Equipment: Thin gym mats, pinny, or bib

Description: Floor mats are spread around the playing area. Choose one or two students to be sharks, and give them a pinny or bib. Other students are sailors, who start the game standing on "ships" (mats). The leader gives the go-ahead for the sailors to "swim," and then the sailors try to run to a new ship without getting tagged by a shark. Sailors who are tagged become sharks and wear a pinny or bib. The game ends when only a few sailors remain; these sailors can be the first sharks when the game starts over.

Adapted from "Sailors and Sharks," PE Central, accessed December 1, 2022, www.pecentral.org/lessonideas/ViewLesson. asp?ID=291.

Adaptations:

- *Simple:* Take the gym mats out of the game. Walking only.
- *Difficult:* Add another shark to the game.

Ollie Ollie Octopus

Description: Participants line up on one side of the playing area. The leader will stand in the middle of the room. Once the leader gives the verbal cue "ollie, ollie, octopus" the participants run from one side of the room to the other without being tagged by the leader (the octopus). If a participant gets tagged by the leader (octopus), then they must then sit down where they were caught. These participants then try to catch other participants from where they are sitting. The game is played until only one participant is left. The last person becomes the octopus. If a participant isn't engaged in the game by being in a less traveled space of the playing area, give the participant a pool noodle for tagging. This gives the participant more chances to tag someone out.

Adapted from "Ollie Ollie Octopus," Fit Kids Healthy Kids, accessed December 1, 2022, https://fkhk.sportmanitoba.ca/node/697.

Adaptations:

- *Simple:* Decrease the playing area. Walking only.
- *Difficult:* Tagged players remain standing and can take one step to tag others.

Note: Be aware of social exclusion where a player is tagged early to reduce that person's involvement or a certain player is never tagged. The instructor may need to lead a discussion on inclusion with the participants.

Treasure Chest

Equipment: Two different-colored Hula-Hoops, beanbags

Description: Two hoops are set up at opposite sides of the playing area. The hoops are different colors to distinguish teams. Beanbags are divided equally between the hoops. Participants are divided into two teams. These two teams each have their own hoop. The beanbags are considered their "treasure." The point of the game is to steal the other team's beanbags in a given amount of time. Participants can decide which locomotor skill to use to move in the space and which will be the most effective in getting the most "treasure."

Adapted from "Treasure Chest," Physed Games, accessed December 1, 2022, www.physedgames.com/treasure-chest/.

Adaptations:

- *Simple:* Set up two hoops: one hoop with beanbags and the other empty. Instruct the participants to pick up and move the beanbags to the empty hoop as fast as they can.
- *Difficult:* Increase the distance between the hoops. Each team is allowed a goalie in front of their hoop in order to decrease the chances of the other team stealing their beanbags.

Ball Tag

Equipment: Ball

Description: A child holds a ball with both hands and must "catch" (tag) the others by running and touching them with the ball. When children are tagged, they take a ball and become catchers themselves. The last child caught begins the next game as the catcher (*Volleyball Canada*, 2017)

Adaptations:

- *Simple:* Use a bigger ball. Decrease the space.
- *Difficult:* Use a smaller ball.

FMS and Sport Skill Games

Red Light, Green Light

Equipment: Green, red, and yellow beanbags

Description: Participants line up in a row. The instructor uses a green and a red beanbag to give a visual cue to participants. The instructor tells participants that when they say green it means go. Red means stop. Hand cues can be used to show stop and go. Participants move from one end of the room to another.

Adapted from "Red Light, Green Light," Playworks, accessed December 21, 2022, www.playworks.org/game-library/red-light-green-light.

Adaptations:
- *Simple:* Decrease the playing space.
- *Difficult:* Add in a yellow beanbag that can be used as a "slow" movement cue. Participants must move slowly in the space.

Chicken Toss

Equipment: Rubber chicken or any rubber animal or fish

Description: Participants sit in a circle. A rubber chicken or any rubber animal can be used. Participants call out or point to the person they are going to throw the rubber chicken to (may need to be prompted by instructor). Participants throw the rubber toy in the circle.

Adaptations:
- *Simple:* Participants can use any throwing motion and use one or two hands.
- *Difficult:* Participants use overhand throwing and can stand in a circle instead of sitting. Spread participants out around the playing area for larger throwing distances.

Scavenger Hunt

Description: Prior to the program put signs around the building with various gross motor tasks on the signs. Have the participants form groups, each with one leader. Participants need to complete all the tasks as a group. This allows the participants to become familiar with each other, the leader, and the building.

Builders and Bulldozers

Equipment: Pylons

Description: Scatter various equipment around the space that can be upright or knocked over (pylons, batons, and so on). Divide the class in two groups: *builders*, who try to keep all equipment upright, and *bulldozers*, who try to knock all equipment down. Students should not use their feet or hit equipment with excessive force. Switch roles so all students have the opportunity to play both roles.

Adapted from "Builders and Bulldozers," The Physical Educator, last modified 2017, www.thephysicaleducator.com/game/builders-bulldozers.

Adaptations:

- *Simple:* Smaller play area or fewer pylons. Walking only.
- *Difficult:* Increase play area and use running as a locomotor skill. Allow one leader or participant to be able to move the pylons around the playing area.

Clean Up

Equipment: Pylons

Description: "Cleaning up" is a simple concept that many participants with ASD can understand. The instructor spreads the pylons out around the playing area and instructs that the participants "clean up" or stack the pylons on top of each other as fast as possible.

Adaptations:

- *Difficult:* Time the activity for 30 seconds or one minute. Children count how many pylons they are able to clean up. Play "beat your score" by having a child see how many more pylons can be accumulated in the next timed period.

End Zone Game

Equipment: An even number of balls

Description: This invasion game can be played with any ball or object to instill defending your zone. The group is divided into two teams. Two teams face each other, and each defends their end. Each team has the same number of balls. At the leader's signal, students roll their ball onto the opponent's side and try to stop incoming balls. Balls that reach the opponent's end zone cannot be replayed. At the leader's second signal, students freeze, and no more balls may be rolled. The team with the fewest balls wins.

Adaptations:
- *Simple:* Reduce the distance between the end zones. Each team has their own color of ball to help distinguish their own team's balls from their opponents' balls.
- *Difficult:* This can be played with soccer balls and dribbling through the opponent's end zone.

Inclusive Community Sports Program: Soccability

There are few inclusive community sport programs for children on the autism spectrum. Yet the benefits on improved motor and social skills of autistic children, improved motor skills of nonautistic children, and positive changes in attitudes toward autistic children have been found as a result of participation in such programs (Sansi et al., 2021). Soccability is an inclusive soccer program for children on the spectrum and their friends to enjoy physical activity in a positive social environment through the sport of soccer. See table 5.2 for an overview of the Soccability program.

Table 5.2   Soccability Program Overview

PROGRAM	SOCCABILITY
Participants	Children 4-14 years with a difference, plus a friend
Length of program	One hour per week for five weeks, May and June
Instructors	Two participants: one staff. Staff, with training in differences, were paired with a soccer expert.
Staff training	Consistent vocabulary, sign language, strategies for anxiety reduction, motivation, and disruptive behavior
Venue	Fenced soccer field to reduce running. No visible distractions.
Uniforms	Children wore their own shirts (either a light or dark shirt). Pinnies were provided to distinguish teams.
Lesson format	Consistent format
Warm-up	Always in the center circle. All children involved.
Groupings	Children were divided by age and motor ability for skill stations and games.
Skill stations	Groups met in the same location each week. Same-color pylons were used to clearly mark areas.
Cool-down	All children came together at the center circle for parachute games.
Program completion	All children received a T-shirt and a team photo.

Conclusion

In summary, games and sports provide an opportunity for children on the spectrum to develop movement skills, learn game strategies, and join with their peers, family, and friends in physical activity. By using the TGfU method in lessons, physical educators can organize the content to transfer skills and tactics across similar games and reduce anxiety for students. From success in physical education, students on the spectrum may join their peers in community sport and recreation programs.

CHAPTER 6

Family and Friends

Children's quality of life is enhanced when they can participate, confidently and competently, in physical activities and games with family and friends. This chapter provides ideas for teaching common activities enjoyed with family and friends. For the purpose of initiating skill development, this chapter will focus on learning to ride a bicycle, skateboard, or scooter; to swim and practice water safety; and to skate. Each skill is presented in a step by step format.

Bike Riding

Learning to ride a bicycle provides many benefits, including an opportunity for physical activity, the ability to participate with family and friends in a social activity, and independent travel on trails and around the block.

Skill: Bike Riding

Length of learning time: two to three times per week for 30 minutes, with assistance and practice at home, for two to four months. Some children may take longer.

Equipment:

- Bicycle
- Helmet
- Bike stand
- Polyspots
- Countdown timer
- Camera to record videos

Step 1: The child simply pushes the bike independently, in a straight line and around pylons or other objects.

Step 2: Place the bike on the stand that supports the child and prevents them from falling over. Encourage the child to sit on the bike to become comfortable with this position. If no stand is available, lower the seat so that the child can place both feet on the ground.

Step 3: With the feet on the ground, start placing hands on the bike. Place stickers on the handlebars and use verbal cue of "touch this."

Step 4: With the bike still on the stand, start placing feet on the pedals and use the verbal cue of "touch this."

Step 5: Once comfortable with both hands and feet on the bike, practice balancing (side to side) on the bike. If using a stand in steps 1 through 4, take the bike off the stand. The leader stands in front holding the handles of the bike while the child puts both feet on the bike. Gradually, the leader releases hands and the child can feel balance.

Step 6: Teach the child to put the feet down when falling. Use the verbal cue of "put foot down on floor" when the leader tilts the bike to one side. The leader can tilt the bike to the left and give the verbal cue "put left foot down." If a child has a struggle day, use a sticky mat or polyspot to indicate where to put the foot down.

Step 7: Use physical prompting and manipulate the child's feet while giving the verbal cue of "push" or "pedal." Take a video to capture pedaling, and show the child doing the movement in the video.

Step 8: Becoming proficient at pedaling takes a lot of practice. To keep children motivated, use countdown strategies through a counting application. Set the counter to 20 seconds, and pedal until the timer counts down. Gradually increase the length of time pedaling.

Step 9: Once the child is able to pedal for a short period of time, place visual cues around the area for the child to pedal to the items. Use a visual schedule to show how many of the items are set out, and the child can choose the order to pedal to each item.

Step 10: Bike riding takes good visual concentration. Cue the child by saying, "Bike goes where the eyes go."

Step 11: The next step is to put straight arms on the handlebars.

Step 12: To learn to squeeze the hand brakes, use the verbal cues of "right" and "left." Use the this-then-that strategy, which specifies to first squeeze right then squeeze left. If motivation is fleeting, use this strategy to practice bike riding first, then play a favorite game.

Step 13: To continue motivation once proficiency is reached, the family can develop social stories combined with images of the child and locations to create bike rides that they could enjoy together (e.g., going for ice cream).

Skateboarding or Scootering

Some children may have a different understanding than other children on the use of play objects and may choose to use an object in a completely different manner. Even when a child on the spectrum may have seen a family member or friend using a skateboard or scooter, they may want to play with it differently.

Skill: Skateboarding or Scootering

Length of learning time: 10 to 20 minutes daily, if possible with assistance and near home so it is easy to do. Requires two to four months, depending on age and ability.

Equipment: Skateboard or scooter

Step 1: Have the child stand on the skateboard with both feet without falling off.

Step 2: Have the child stand, and use physical prompting to place one foot on the board and the other on the ground.

Step 3: Use physical prompting to push the foot on the ground allowing the child to go in the forward motion.

Step 4: Encourage the child to use correct footing where the opposite foot to dominant arm is forward and the nondominant foot is pushing off the ground.

Step 5: Try to have the child push off the ground. A flat surface for more hesitant participants and a slight downhill for the more adventurous. This needs to be a more fluid movement and done with confidence. Look for an area clear of debris or small rocks, which can cause the skateboarder to fall.

Step 6: Once the child is moving well, try to get them to shift their front foot sideways as well as bringing their pushing-off foot up onto the board. This can be the most difficult part to learn, but keep motivation high in order for success.

Step 7: Practice turns by leaning. Have a parent or teacher hold their hands and move down a slight hill, cueing the child to lean left and right, with the parent or teacher also leaning to give the visual cue.

Step 8: Practice stopping. Most children will just jump off, but one can practice while holding hand in hand and having the child push the back foot down and back to stop. This is called a tail stop. Most skateboards have a plastic stopper on the back to help you stop.

Swimming and Water Safety

Many children on the autism spectrum like water. They like the pressure of water on their bodies. Water, however, can cause serious injury or drowning when a child has no fear, swimming ability, or understanding of water safety. Every child needs to learn to swim.

Skill: Swimming

Length of learning time: 20 to 45 minutes per session

Equipment:

- Life jacket
- Pool noodles or floaters
- Pool toys (e.g., buckets or watering can)
- Small toys that float

Step 1: Sitting on the edge of the pool or on a step of the pool so the upper body is not submerged. Spending time getting comfortable with splashing and playing in the water. Attempting to get lower and more submerged in the water.

Step 2: Standing in the pool. Practice activities similar to those in the previous step. Attempt to put face in water for blowing bubbles.

Step 3: Moving in the pool (walking, splashing, bouncing, high knees).

Step 4: Hold onto the wall and practice kicking your feet with straight legs. Practice little and big kicks in the pool.

Step 5: Hold onto the wall and practice kicks with a floater or pool noodle.

Step 6: Practice floating on the back.

Step 7: Practice floating on the front.

Step 8: Practice favorite float and try moving and kicking legs in order to move in the water. Use a floater board to decrease difficulty.

Step 9: While standing in the water, practice moving your arms in a circular motion. Practice keeping the fingers together while moving the arms.

Step 10: Practice favorite float again and try kicking legs and moving arms at the same time in order to move in the pool. To increase motivation, add a toy or floater for the person to swim to.

Ice Skating

Ice skating is a difficult skill to master. In northern climates, skating and games involving skating provide many opportunities for physical activity with family and friends.

Skill: Ice Skating

Length of learning time: The length of time can be dependent on multiple factors including the frequency with which the person is able to get onto the ice as well as the length of time spent on the ice. Skates can be quite uncomfortable in the beginning, so the student may take awhile getting used to the skates and not stay on the ice for very long. Ideally one could practice skating for 30 minutes every day for two weeks, but a weekly lesson of an hour can also work as long as the student is motivated.

Equipment:

- Soft-shell, size-appropriate skates
- Helmet
- Hockey sticks or learn-to-skate apparatus

Step 1: Learn balance on skates by walking and marching on the skates. A balance apparatus can be used, but, ideally, try not to use one.

Step 2: Find inner edge and practice gliding on the inner edge.

Step 3: Find outer edge and practice gliding on the outer edge.

Step 4: Move from inner and outer edge until smoother movement.

Step 5: Use the push and glide movement to move from inner and outer edge.

Step 6: Attempt to increase ease of transitioning from inner and outer edge.

Step 7: Practice stopping on the ice by using the "snow plow" in order to slow down. The snow plow technique makes a "V" with the skates by bringing toes together and heels to the outside.

Step 8: Increase speed, endurance, and ability to change directions and stop quickly.

Conclusion

In summary, children's quality of life is enhanced when they can play with friends and family. Bike riding, skateboarding, swimming, and ice skating are common physical activities. While learning these skills may take some time and practice, the opportunity to participate with friends and family makes it worthwhile.

Grayson's Story

One of my favorite memories involves a young man named Grayson, who was part of our adapted kids triathlon group. We trained for four months ahead of the community kids triathlon as a small group of four students and four leaders. We trained twice a week, incorporating biking and running (mostly running and stopping) and swimming every other week. Each child had their own distances they were training for, but Grayson, being the oldest, had the most to swim and the longest to run and bike. Race day was a very busy day, and each child had their own leader with them to help them from getting out of the pool and immediately onto their bike. We had practiced being wet and then getting onto a bike prior because this experience isn't a fun one for anyone, especially someone with sensory issues. Grayson completed his swim and was running out with his leader to his bike with all of the chaos of other kids and their parents cheering them on. He asked me how many laps he had to bike. I said three laps. I cheered him on for two but then found out that because he was older, it was now four laps. I saw Grayson coming in on the bike and was yelling to keep going. He looked at me very confused, but his leader led him on to his fourth lap. I could hear him arguing with the leader about the number of laps as he came in to start the running portion. I could still hear him as he was running the path, complaining about the number of laps, and as he crossed the finish line of his first triathlon, much to the happiness and pride of all involved, he was still very mad at me for not giving him the correct number of laps. He was solely focused on the number of laps being incorrect and not that he had just completed a triathlon. I felt absolute pride for him as well as such guilt for getting the information wrong and making his moment not as joyous. This is why I truly love working with individuals on the spectrum, because you never know how any events will play out. I have learned so much, especially how to make an adaptation in the moment in order to achieve the best outcome for each child. In this example, I made the mistake that caused the participant to have to change and adapt in order to succeed.

Erin Bennett

Fitness

Children and adults alike need to maintain an active lifestyle. This can be especially important for reducing anxiety, burning energy, increasing bone density and muscle development, improving cardiovascular development, and enhancing overall health for an individual. Fitness activities can be learned as a child and continued into adulthood. Some children will enjoy fitness activities more than other types of physical activity and games. It is sometimes more enjoyable to a child on the spectrum because fitness can be a solo activity that they will typically have control of (speed or length of time), and they can usually listen to their music or watch a show while doing it. Fitness activities can provide the child with the strength and endurance for enjoyable family and community activities, such as bike riding or skating.

This chapter describes some instructional considerations and tools. The fitness activities of walking, treadmills, weight training at home and school, gaming, online and virtual fitness classes, outdoor equipment, and weight training at fitness centers are presented here.

Fitness In and Outside School

Participating in fitness opportunities while in school is very important, because physical education class is not always a positive experience. Some students may lack the gross motor skills and understanding of how to play sports or efficiently move their bodies. By participating in fitness activities, youth can develop their cardiovascular endurance and locomotor movements in a variety of environments. Students who have previously not been active participants in physical education may find that fitness meets their activity needs with programs they can do at their own pace. Using cardiovascular machines, such as a treadmill or a stationary bike, students are able to set their time and effort level. They are also able to watch shows or listen to music while doing the exercise, which can increase motivation. They can also use indoor weight machines or outdoor exercise equipment at their own pace and effort level.

Using physical fitness as part of a student's individualized education plan can be a vital part of the student's overall well-being. It can also give the student credit for physical education if they are not actively participating in school. At the junior high and high school level, most schools have a fitness facility on school grounds, where students can do their own program during the physical education period. If there isn't a fitness facility on site, one may be able to arrange a program at a community facility and still receive credit for physical education.

Engaging in their community by participating in recreation and fitness centers and outdoor fitness equipment provides a sense of community for the child or youth and their family. They may not have been able to be a part of a "team" prior, so being part of a fitness facility can be a major milestone for an individual and their family. Starting the transition to a fitness center while still in school creates a routine and a sense of familiarity for the student, which can continue after they have left school. These healthy habits formed in school can continue as they grow into young adults. Fitness activities provide a great community experience for the student and may be something they can do together with their family.

Instructional Considerations and Tools

Begin by teaching the basic fitness skills that can be done by an individual. These skills include cardiovascular skills, such as walking, running, stair climbing, or even strength training, such as push-ups and squats. Agility and balance skills are also important to practice for lifelong health. These activities can be used for the rest of their lives; therefore, it is important to engage the person in the process of selecting the activities. Provide opportunities and choice for activities that are of interest. If their home will be used for fitness, decide together how to set up the environment and where the fitness equipment and exercise will take place. When using technology for fitness, use the technology that the student is familiar with to increase communication in a new situation for the student. This will also make the individual more comfortable in an uncomfortable situation, which can promote adherence to the new activity.

Social Stories

A social story, as described in chapter 3, can be developed to introduce the idea of any of the fitness activities described in this chapter. The social story can break down the actual exercises or describe the setup and schedule of going to a fitness facility. A social story can also be used to introduce the idea of doing fitness in the home.

Visual Schedules

A visual schedule can also be on a tablet or phone, which allows a sense of sameness for a youth because it is commonplace to carry a cell phone or tablet around in day-to-day activities. The youth can be shown their workout routine at home or at a local fitness center as a visual schedule on a tablet, and they can then complete the routine independently. The leader takes photos of the youth doing the required exercises and puts the photos into a scheduler program, which will then create an easier visual schedule. The youth will now be able to carry the handheld device or tablet in the fitness facility and be able to understand what to do and where to go in order to complete their workout. This also makes it easier for multiple individuals to help the youth with their program because they do not need to be overly familiar with the program nor the facility. The visual schedule also allows the youth to become more independent in completing their exercise program. With a camera typically being available in these tablets or devices, one can easily add new activities, people, or locations.

Timers and Set Repetitions

Try using a timer or a set number of repetitions of each exercise so that the student knows how long their workout will be.

Charts

Use a chart that the student can put a sticker or checkmark on each time an exercise is done or a full workout is completed in order to gain access to an activity or reward that motivates the student. For example, when 10 workouts are completed, they earn a bigger reward.

Questions to Ask

The following are some questions to ask at the fitness center to facilitate a smoother transition to training for a student.

1. *What are the social expectations and behavior at this fitness center?* A fitness center may be a new environment that a youth may not be used to, so things such as gym etiquette may need to be reviewed or written out prior to their first visits to the facility. This could include waiting their turn for equipment or wiping off machines or equipment after use.

2. *What is the environment like?* Bright lights and loud music are typical in most fitness facilities, and there can be larger groups of people in the workout area. These elements can all cause an individual to be uncomfortable in this environment. As mentioned earlier, choosing a less busy time at the fitness facility or working out in a quieter section of the gym can help. Midafternoon could be the best time because it is typically less busy and would still fall within school hours.

3. *What should we discuss with the staff?* Be sure to discuss with the facility staff the student's diverse needs so they are aware if there are any differences in behaviors. Address concerns about the student having an adult with them if they are under the age of 16. A familiar face for the student at the front desk and in the fitness center if they have any issues or concerns can provide comfort and reduce anxiety. Locations of the change rooms, water fountains, and cleaning products are also important to teach through social stories, videos, and at the site. Be sure to inform the staff if students require their cell phones for their programs.

4. *How accessible is the building?* It is important to assess if the facility is easily accessible in that the student can either walk or take transportation to the facility. If the parking lot is far away from the facility, it can lower the student's motivation to do their workout.

5. *Is there any adapted equipment?* Some adapted equipment, such as a hand crank or weight machines that are able to have the seat removed to accommodate a wheelchair, may be needed.

6. *May the student bring others for the workout?* The student could do their workout with siblings or parents because this can be motivating. Using respite staff can also work. Finding a friend to work out with the student can be even more motivating and can also be good practice for social interactions and develop-

ing meaningful relationships outside their family unit. When seeking a personal trainer or fitness instructor, make sure it is a good fit and that the trainer understands the student and their needs as well as what motivates them. They need to provide a structured environment that doesn't change too often without warning as well as a familiarity and continuity each time students attend a workout or class.

Activities

Fitness begins with a warm-up to prepare the body and mind for the upcoming activity. The goal is to strengthen and stretch the muscles for healthy development. Activities can include weight training, gaming, outdoor equipment, and classes.

Warm-Ups

All fitness activities begin with a warm-up. Warm-ups involve gradually increasing one's movements and increasing the heart rate. The muscles and joints that will be used in the fitness activity should be moved with increasing velocity through their range of motion. This can be as easy as marching in place, jogging on the spot, or just simply walking around the gym or facility or even outside. If the person is comfortable they could use the treadmill or bike.

Weight Training

It is important to set out a structured routine for each workout, whether it is at home or in a fitness facility (see figure 7.1). Keep goals small and increase every few weeks. Cardio machines can be used to motivate the student; for example, by suggesting 10 minutes today and then next week 12 minutes. Set goals for exercise repetition and sets that are challenging enough for the student. Use equipment and machines that are motivating for the student. Have a basic understanding of machines and how to properly set them up without risk of injury. Use a cell phone to set up a workout guideline, and take pictures of each machine or piece of equipment so that the student knows how to use them. This can increase their independence in the gym because they are in control of their own program, and they look like everyone else using a phone at the gym.

Gaming

Another excellent way to engage a child in physical activity at home is by using video games, such as Wii. Not only do the video games provide some fitness benefits but they will also assist the child with learning the movements and actions of different sports and activities. With communication from the physical education teacher, a child can prepare at home for what specific sport or goals they are working toward in physical education class.

There is a large selection of game systems and games available for any sport or fitness activity. These games will help children become familiar with and even master the basic skills required to participate in activities that are going on at school, in the community, or with family and friends. A child gains confidence when they are able to move their body

Sample Visual Program

Home or gym program

Equipment: dumbbells, exercise bands, exercise loops, mat
Warm-up: five minutes of light cardiovascular activity, such as marching or jumping jacks

MUSCLE AREA	EXERCISE	SETS	REPS
Chest	Push-up		
Back	Exercise band row		
Shoulders	Exercise band shoulder press		
Biceps	Biceps curls with bands		
Triceps	Dips on a bench		
Quadriceps	Squats		
Hamstrings	Exercise bands deadlift		
Glutes	Glute raise		
Core	Plank		
Core	Sit-ups		
High intensity cardiovascular	20/10 Tabata of cardio exercises (20 sec work, 10 sec rest)		

Equipment: weight machines
Warm-up: 5 to 10 minutes on a cardiovascular machine, such as a treadmill or stationary bike

MUSCLE AREA	EXERCISE	SETS	REPS
Chest	Chest press machine		
Back	Lat pulldown		
Shoulders	Shoulder press machine		
Biceps	Biceps curl machine		
Triceps	Triceps extension machine		
Quadriceps	Leg press		
Hamstrings	Lying leg curl		
Glutes	Hip thrust machine		
Core	Abdominal machine		
Back	Back extension bench		
High intensity cardiovascular	Done on a cardiovascular machine 20 /10 Tabata (20 sec work, 10 sec rest)		

FIGURE 7.1

the way they need to in order to perform the actions required to participate in a specific activity. Video games allow them to perform an action repeatedly and also give some results for accuracy of the movement. The picture on the screen will also give them an image of what the atmosphere looks like prior to participating in the actual activity or venue.

Outdoor Equipment

Some community parks have instructions written on equipment in the park, telling people how to use the equipment as a fitness training session. Many personal trainers take their clients to local parks to do their sessions. There are a number of benefits to exercising outdoors, such as connecting with nature, breathing in fresh air, and being in a motivational and inspiring place. Children and youth with sensory sensitivities may not enjoy the overstimulation that can occur indoors. The outdoor environment provides wide open spaces, a quieter atmosphere, and calmer visual stimulation. Supervision is important to ensure safety, and precautions should be taken, such as drinking enough water to keep the body temperature cool and wearing sunscreen as needed.

Online and Virtual Fitness Classes

Another option that can be used with children and youth is to take advantage of the virtual fitness classes that can be offered by DVD, video game systems, online, or within the gym itself. Some gyms are using large-screen setups in the group fitness rooms to offer members an option to participate in a fitness class during off hours. If the child does not wish to attend a gym, these programs can be completed in the comforts of the child's home. This is a good option to help integrate someone into participating in an actual fitness class. It is very intimidating for many people to enter a room full of people and take part in a class they have never attended. The option of going into a fitness center at a quiet time of the day and having only one or two people participate in a class led by a virtual instructor removes the initial intimidation of other people. When a person is able to get used to the atmosphere at the gym during quiet times, practice their skills, and even seek help from staff at the gym, it prepares them to take things a step further. Once their confidence level and grasp of skills increase, they may feel ready to join a regular class.

Conclusion

In summary, fitness activities contribute to the health of children and youth but also improve quality of life. Opportunities for community, friends, and family to become more involved in the person's life on a different level are another benefit of participating in a fitness program.

John was a member of the YMCA and had been coming to the fitness center for about a year with his respite worker. She reached out to me after a year because she knew I had been adapting programs for younger children there at that time. She wanted him to have a specific program and to try new things, because he liked to stay on the elliptical machine for the entire hour. John was in his early twenties. I showed him the weight machines and how to adjust them and set the weights. I like the weight machines as an introduction to weight training because it is a simple way to get a full-body workout, and typically the machines are all numbered or in a circuit on the gym floor, so it is a clear plan for the person. Taking a picture of John on each machine and of the weight setting allowed John to become independent in only a short number of weeks. He used his cell phone to look at the pictures and knew which machine was next and the weight setting needed. He looks like every other member working out in the gym who carries their phone with them, so it isn't an obvious tool that may make him feel self-conscious. Over time and with practice with the iPad, I was able to take a photo of him doing new exercises, which then allowed me to add in a couple of core exercises that are done on a mat, and I even added in some tubing exercises. The tubing is available only at the front desk of the YMCA, so I took a picture of the front desk and then of the tubing so that in his program he knew to go to the front desk first to ask for the tubing before he began his exercise program. I then printed out the pictures with a set of short instructions, similar to a social story used for younger children, so he could look at it before he came to the gym and then would have his phone on him in the gym for reference.

Erin Bennett

Adams, D., MacDonald, L., & Keen, D. (2019). Teacher responses to anxiety-related behaviours in students on the autism spectrum. *Research in Developmental Disabilities, 86*, 11-19.

Alberta Soccer (2018). Donkey tails. https://albertasoccer.com/wp-content/uploads/2018/01/GrassrootsSessionsToolkitFINAL.pdf

Allen, K.E., Paasche, C.L., Langford R., & Nolan, K. (2011). *Inclusion in early childhood programs: Children with exceptionalities* (5th Canadian ed.). Nelson Education.

American Psychological Association. (2013). *Diagnostic and statistical manual of mental disorders* (5th ed.). APA.

Bejerot, S., Edgar, J., & Humble, M. (2011). Poor performance in physical education: A risk factor for bully victimization. A case-control study. *Acta Paediatrica, 100*(3), 413-419.

Bhat, A.N., Landa, R.J., & Galloway, J.C. (2011). Current perspectives on motor functioning in infants, children, and adults with autism spectrum disorders. *Physical Therapy, 91*(7), 1116-1129.

Bottema-Beutel, K., Kapp, S.K., Nester, J.N., Sasson, N.J., & Hand, B.N. (2020). Avoiding ableist language: Suggestions for autism researchers. *Autism in Adulthood*. https://doi.org/10.1089/aut.2020.0014

Boulton, K. (n.d.) *Line tag*. https://elementarypegames.weebly.com/line-tag.html

Canadian Society for Exercise Physiology (CSEP). (2021). Early years (0-4 years): Infants, toddlers and preschoolers. In *Canadian 24-Hour Movement Guidelines: An Integration of Physical Activity, Sedentary Behaviour, and Sleep*. https://csepguidelines.ca

Cunningham, M. (2020). "This school is 100% not autistic friendly!" Listening to the voices of primary-aged autistic children to understand what an autistic friendly primary school should be like. *International Journal of Inclusive Education, 26*(12), 1211-1225. https://doi.org/10.1080/13603116.2020.1789767

Definition of Adapted Physical Activity. (n.d.). International Federation of Adapted Physical Activity. https://ifapa.net/definition

Edelson, S.M. (1999). Overview of Autism. *Education, 36*(3), 45-48.

Fit Kids Healthy Kids. (2021a). Balloon Badminton. https://fkhk.sportmanitoba.ca/node/143

Fit Kids Healthy Kids. (2021b). Ollie, Ollie, Octopus. https://fkhk.sportmanitoba.ca/node/697

Fletcher-Watson, S., & Happe, F. (2019). *Autism: An introduction to psychological theory and current debate*. Routlege Taylor & Francis Group. https://doi.org/10.4324/9781315101699

Floorcurl. (2022). How to play. https://floorcurl.com/how-to-play

Fraser, L. (2005). *Plan for small stuff and sweat* [Unpublished manuscript]. Orchard Park Secondary School, Hamilton, ON.

Gilchrist, K.H., Hegarty-Craver, M., Christian, R.B., Grego, S., Kies, A.C., & Wheeler, A.C. (2018). Automated detection of repetitive motor behaviors as an outcome measurement in intellectual and developmental disabilities. *Journal of Autism and Developmental Disorders, 48*(5), 1458-1466. https://doi.org/10.1007/s10803-017-3408-6

Gray, C. (2004). Social stories 10.0: The new defining criteria and guidelines. *Jenison Autism Journal, 15,* 2-21.

Green, J., Pickles, A., Pasco, G., Bedford, R., Wan, M.W., Elsabbagh, M., Slonims, V., Gliga, T., Jones, E., Cheung, C., Charman, T., Johnson, M., & British Autism Study of Infant Siblings (BASIS) Team (2017). Randomised trial of a parent-mediated intervention for infants at high risk for autism: longitudinal outcomes to age 3 years. *Journal of Child Psychology and Psychiatry, and Allied Disciplines, 58*(12), 1330-1340. https://doi.org/10.1111/jcpp.12728

Griffin, L., & Butler, J. (Eds.). (2005). *Teaching games for understanding: Theory, research and practice.* Human Kinetics.

Haydn-Davies, D. (2005). How does the concept of physical literacy relate to what is and what could be the practice of physical education? *British Journal of Teaching Physical Education, 36*(3), 45-48.

Hilton, C.L., Zhang, Y., Whilte, M.R., Klohr, C.L., & Constantino, J. (2012). Motor impairment in sibling pairs concordant and discordant for autism spectrum disorders. *Autism, 16*(4), 430-441.

Hopper, T. (1998). Teaching games-centred games using progressive principles of play. *CAHPERD, 64*(3), 4-7.

Humphrey, N., & Lewis, S. (2008). "Make me normal": The views and experiences of pupils on the autistic spectrum in mainstream secondary schools. *Autism, 12*(1), 23-46. https://doi.org/10.1177/1362361307085267

Hundley, R.J., Shui, A., & Malow, B.A. (2016). Relationship between subtypes of restricted and repetitive behaviors and sleep disturbance in autism spectrum disorder. *Journal of Autism and Developmental Disorders, 46,* 3448-3457. https://doi.org/10.1007/s10803-016-2884-4

Johnson, C.P. (2004). Early clinical characteristics of children with autism. In V.B. Gupta (Ed.), *Autistic spectrum disorders in children* (pp. 86-121). Marcel Dekker.

Kapp, S.K. (Ed.). (2020). *Autistic community and the neurodiversity movement: Stories from the frontline.* Palgrave MacMillan.

Kasser, S.L., & Lytle, R. (2013). *Inclusive physical activity: Promoting health for a lifetime* (2nd ed.). Human Kinetics.

Kirk, D., & MacPhail, A. (2002) Teaching games for understanding and situated learning: Rethinking the Bunker-Thorpe model. *Journal of Teaching in Physical Education, 21,* 177-192.

Lee, B. (2004). *Parental values and concerns about participation in physical activity by persons with intellectual disabilities* (Publication No. 3158965) [Doctoral dissertation, Michigan State University]. ProQuest Dissertations.

Long Term Development (2019). Sport for Life. https://sportforlife.ca/wp-content/uploads/2019/06/Long-Term-Development-in-Sport-and-Physical-Activity-3.0.pdf

Lord, C., Risi, S., DiLavore, P.S., Shulman, C., Thurm, A., & Pickles, A. (2006). Autism from 2 to 9 years of age. *Archives of General Psychiatry, 63*(6), 694-701.

McClannahan, L.E., & Krantz, P. (2010). *Activity schedules for children with autism: Teaching independent behavior* (2nd ed.). Bethesda, MD: Woodbine House.

Muhle, R.A., Reed, H.E., Stratigos, K.A., & Veenstra-VanderWeele, J. (2018) The emerging clinical neuroscience of autism spectrum disorder: A review. *JAMA Psychiatry, 75*(5), 514-523. https://doi.org/10.1001/jamapsychiatry.2017.4685

NCCP Fundamental Movement Skills. (2018). Community Leader Workshop–Coach Workbook Coaching Association of Canada.

NCCP Fundamental Movement Skills. (2009). Community Leader Workshop–Reference Material Version 1.0. Coaching Association of Canada.

Ochtabienski, S. (2012). *A+ activity* [Unpublished manuscript].

O'Connor, J., French, R., & Henderson, H. (2000). Use of physical activity to improve behavior of children with autism—two for one benefits. *Palaestra, 16*, 22-29.

Pan, C.Y. (2008). Objectively measured physical activity between children with autism spectrum disorders and children without disabilities during inclusive recess settings in Taiwan. *Journal of Autism and Developmental Disorders, 38*(7),1292-1301. https://doi.org/10.1007/s10803-007-0518-6

PE Central. (2016). Sharks and sailors. www.pecentral.org/lessonideas/ViewLesson.asp?ID=291

PE Central. (2017). Statues at the museum. www.pecentral.org/lessonideas/ViewLesson.asp?ID=133201#.YmtklS971Z0

Physed Games. (2022). Treasure chest. https://physedgames.com/treasure-chest

Physical Educator. (2017). Builders and bulldozers. https://thephysicaleducator.com/game/builders-bulldozers

Playworks. (2022a). Red light. Green light. www.playworks.org/game-library/red-light-green-light

Playworks. (2022b). Wall ball. www.playworks.org/game-library/wall-ball

Reid, G., O'Connor, J., & Lloyd, M. (2003). The autism spectrum disorders, physical activity instruction—part III. *Palaestra, 19*(2), 20-26, 47.

Rouse, P. (2009). *Inclusion in physical education*. Human Kinetics.

Sanders, S.W. (2002). *Active for life. Developmentally appropriate movement programs for young children*. National Association for the Education of Young Children, Washington, DC. Human Kinetics.

Sandt, D. (2008). Social stories for students with autism in physical education. *Journal of Physical Education, Recreation and Dance, 79*(6), 42-45.

Sansi, A., Nalbant, S., & Ozer, D. (2021). Effects of an inclusive physical activity program on the motor skills, social skills and attitudes of students with and without autism spectrum disorder. *Journal of Autism and Developmental Disorders, 51*(7), 2254-2270. https://doi.org/10.1007/s10803-020-04693-z

Sport for Life. (2016). *Developing physical literacy: A guide for parents of children ages 0-12.* https://sportforlife.ca/wp-content/uploads/2016/12/DPL_ENG_Feb29.indd_.pdf

Stopka, C. (2006). *Teachers survival guidebook.* PE Central.

Trost, S.G. (2007). Active Education: Physical education, physical activity and academic performance. Active Living Research. San Diego State University.

Ultimate Camp Resource. (n.d.). Ship to shore. www.ultimatecampresource.com/camp-games/large-group-games/ship-shore

Volleyball Canada. (2017). *Elementary volleyball teacher guide.* Coaching Association of Canada and Volleyball Canada.

What Is a Social Story? (2022). Carol Gray Social Stories. https://carolgraysocialstories.com/social-stories/what-is-it

What Is Physical Literacy? (2022). Physical Literacy. https://physicalliteracy.ca/physical-literacy

Yanardag, M., Yilmaz, I., & Aras, O. (2010). Approaches to the teaching exercise and sports for the children with autism. *International Journal of Early Childhood Special Education, 2*(3), 214-230.

About the Authors

Erin Bennett is the owner of APAC Lethbridge, which provides adapted physical activity programs for children, youths, and adults of all ability levels in the Lethbridge community. Erin also provides specialized adapted physical education programs for students in the Lethbridge public school district.

Erin, a recipient of an Erasmus Mundus scholarship, received a master's degree in adapted physical activity from the Katholieke Universiteit–Leuven in Belgium and completed her bachelor's degree in physical education from the University of Alberta. At the University of Alberta, Erin worked at the Steadward Centre, which is a specialized center for adapted physical activity founded by Dr. Robert Steadward.

Mary Dyck, PhD, is a retired kinesiology instructor from the University of Lethbridge in Alberta, Canada. She taught adapted physical activity for 10 years. During that time, Mary expanded community adapted activity programs as program codirector for Soccability and manager for the Lethbridge wheelchair basketball program. She was the manager for the Canadian deaf indoor volleyball and beach volleyball program that competed at the Deaflympics from 2015 to 2023. She was inducted into the Lethbridge Sports Hall of Fame as a Builder in 2020. She has coauthored two books—*Everybody Move* and *Coaching Volleyball Champions: Principles and Practices of Successful Coaches.* Mary has 30 years of experience coaching children, coaching athletes in university and provincial programs, and facilitating coaching clinics in volleyball and soccer.

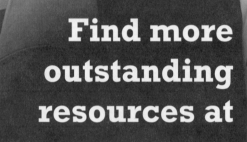